*Poetry in Motion*

# Co Antrim
## Edited by Chris Hallam

 Young**Writers**

First published in Great Britain in 2004 by:
Young Writers
Remus House
Coltsfoot Drive
Peterborough
PE2 9JX
Telephone: 01733 890066
Website: www.youngwriters.co.uk

SB ISBN 1 84460 335 0

# Foreword

This year, the Young Writers' 'Poetry In Motion' competition proudly presents a showcase of the best poetic talent selected from over 40,000 up-and-coming writers nation-wide.

Young Writers was established in 1991 to promote the reading and writing of poetry within schools and to the youth of today. Our books nurture and inspire confidence in the ability of young writers and provide a snapshot of poems written in schools and at home by budding poets of the future.

The thought effort, imagination and hard work put into each poem impressed us all and the task of selecting poems was a difficult but nevertheless enjoyable experience.

We hope you are as pleased as we are with the final selection and that you and your family continue to be entertained with *Poetry In Motion Co Antrim* for many years to come.

# Contents

Michael Donnelly  (13)                               42
Rachael Hunter  (14)                                 42


## Ballyclare High School
Alex Scott  (14)                                     43
James Smyth  (14)                                    44
Christopher Williamson  (12)                         44
Lauren Foster  (15)                                  45
Alan Finlay  (14)                                    46
Rebecca Hamilton  (13)                               46
Emma Montgomery  (15)                                47
Sarah Tilbury  (13)                                  48
Emma Wilson  (14)                                    49
Jenna Hamilton  (14)                                 50
Kim Montgomery  (14)                                 51
Jennifer Dunn  (17)                                  52
Alison Crothers  (11)                                52
Heather Bailie  (17)                                 53
Grace Kennedy  (12)                                  53
Ryan Cooke  (12)                                     54
Nicola Louise Rodgers  (13)                          55
Dawn Comins  (12)                                    55
Matthew Hunter  (12)                                 56
Scott Wylie  (12)                                    56
Emma Jayne Ferguson  (13)                            57
Rachel Smyth  (12)                                   58
Joanne Williamson  (12)                              58
Ashleigh Holmes  (12)                                59
Joanna Caldwell  (17)                                59
Suzanne Weir  (13)                                   60
Caroline Montgomery  (17)                            61
James Bones  (11)                                    61
Ryan Glass  (13)                                     62
Adam Sharratt  (14)                                  63
Emma Gault  (11)                                     63
Chris McNeill  (14)                                  64
Catherine Vennard  (14)                              65
Matthew Lok  (11)                                    65
John Millar  (16)                                    66
Claire Gaffney  (14)                                 67
Edmund Davis  (15)                                   68

David Mairs  (11)                        68
William Andrews  (16)                    69
Jayne Cluff  (14)                        70
Adrian Hughes  (12)                      70
Zoë Scott  (11)                          71
Alex Hagan  (11)                         71
Graeme Farquhar  (11)                    72
Ruth Young  (12)                         72
Stuart Crawford  (12)                    73
Rosie Ramsey  (11)                       73
Emma McAllister  (12)                    74
Rebecca Archbold  (11)                   74
Trevor McClintock  (12)                  75
Daryl Dundee  (11)                       75
Christopher Craig  (11)                  76
Ross D Vint                              77
Rachel Brown  (11)                       77
Catriona Luney  (11)                     78
Rachael Bailie  (11)                     79
Kyle Clarke  (12)                        80
Lee Coupe  (13)                          80
Andrew Mahon  (15)                       81
Jordan Watson  (11)                      81
Jonathan Steenson  (14)                  82
Jane McAllister  (15)                    83
Michael Carson  (14)                     84
Kyle Patterson  (13)                     84
Suzanne Whan  (12)                       85
Nicola Abernethy  (12)                   86
Julie McCormick  (15)                    87
Glenn McMaster  (12)                     88
Craig Reed  (12)                         89

**Belfast Royal Academy**
Danielle McIlwaine  (11)                 89
Danielle Magee  (14)                     90
Steven Laverty  (13)                     91
Nicole Edwards  (11)                     92
Daniel Rice  (14)                        92
Edward Duffy  (14)                       93
David Costley  (11)                      93

## Cambridge House Grammar School
Ruth Barr  (14)                                                     94

## Cross And Passion College
Claire McAuley  (16)                                               95

## Crumlin High School
Emma Dickson  (12)                                                 95
Michael Rees  (12)                                                 96
Sarah Campbell  (12)                                               96
Brendan Scollay  (11)                                              97
Robert McCallister  (11)                                           97
Alistair McKnight  (11)                                            98
Laura Ross  (11)                                                   98
Andrea Hurley  (12)                                                99
Emily Wakeling  (11)                                               99
Georgie Brown  (12)                                               100
Stephanie Patterson  (12)                                         100
Michelle Price  (11)                                              101
April Ingram  (11)                                                101
Thomas McDonnell  (11)                                            102
Jemma Greenberg  (12)                                             102
Luke Campbell  (11)                                               103
David Ingram  (11)                                                103
Liam Murphy  (11)                                                 104
Ethan Stewart  (11)                                               104
Scott Adams  (11)                                                 105
Neil Butler  (11)                                                 105
Jack Deegan  (11)                                                 106
Elizabeth Churton  (11)                                           106
Mark McBride  (11)                                                107
Olya McCambridge  (13)                                            107
Ben Cormican  (11)                                                108
Lucy Best  (11)                                                   108
Christopher Madden  (11)                                          109
Ben Galloway  (11)                                                109
Ian Kirkland  (12)                                                110
Stuart Coulter  (12)                                              110
Karl Taylor  (11)                                                 111
Jodie Cassidy  (11)                                               111

## Cullybackey High School

| | |
|---|---|
| Sammyjo Sloan (13) | 112 |
| Stacey Johnston (13) | 112 |
| Stacey McNeill (13) | 112 |
| Stacey Boardman (12) | 113 |
| Alison Simpson (12) | 113 |
| Gavin Steele (13) | 113 |
| Melissa McCollum (13) | 114 |
| Lee Wilson (12) | 114 |
| William McIntosh (13) | 114 |
| Helen Shaw (12) | 115 |
| Mark Kilpatrick (13) | 115 |

## Dominican College

| | |
|---|---|
| Dearbhlagh Moore (12) | 115 |
| Claire Mullan (13) | 116 |
| Annaliese McCrisken (13) | 117 |
| Hayley Russell (13) | 118 |
| Jessica Turner (13) | 119 |
| Sarah Cochrane (14) | 119 |
| Maeve Corrigan (14) | 120 |
| Rachel MacDonald (14) | 121 |
| Louise Armstrong (14) | 122 |
| Roslyn Cooke (13) | 122 |
| Mary McCaughey (18) | 123 |
| Emma Wilson (14) | 123 |
| Sarah Faloon (11) | 124 |
| Aíne Rogan (11) | 125 |
| Kerri-Louise Murray (11) | 126 |
| Mary McGurk (12) | 127 |
| Nuala Meehan (14) | 128 |
| Nuala Stewart (11) | 129 |
| Bríd McGuinness (13) | 129 |
| Theresa Shields (13) | 130 |
| Niamh McCallin (14) | 130 |
| Sharon Mullan (18) | 131 |
| Kathleen McCoey | 131 |
| Claire Glover (14) | 132 |
| Aoife Kelly (14) | 133 |
| Catherine McCann (14) | 134 |
| Aine Gallagher (15) | 135 |

## Orangefield High School

| | |
|---|---|
| Natalia McConnell (11) | 157 |
| Leah Reid (13) | 157 |
| Claire Jackson (14) | 158 |
| Gemma Albert (12) | 158 |
| Ryan McCormack (14) | 159 |
| Nicola McNeill (13) | 159 |
| David Ross (14) | 160 |
| Jonathan Albert (12) | 160 |
| Leah Spiers (11) | 161 |
| Christopher Hutchinson (13) | 161 |

## Parkhall College

| | |
|---|---|
| Janine Ingram (13) | 162 |
| Rachel Arthur (12) | 162 |
| Donna Cooper (13) | 163 |
| Robert Graham (12) | 163 |
| Angela Lynch (13) | 164 |
| Toni McCrubb (12) | 164 |
| Stacey McLaughlin (13) | 165 |
| Jamie Steele (12) | 166 |
| Glenn Galloway (12) | 166 |
| Grant Simpson (12) | 167 |
| Adam Coyle (12) | 167 |
| Samantha Milligan (12) | 168 |
| Simon Adams (12) | 168 |

## St Louise's College, Belfast

| | |
|---|---|
| Roisin Higgins (11) | 169 |
| Ashling McCabe (11) | 169 |
| Kerriann Nesbitt (11) | 170 |
| Orlaith Lynn (12) | 170 |
| Anna Growcott (11) | 171 |
| Roisin Campbell | 171 |
| Jennifer McConnell (11) | 172 |
| Denilee Vianzon (11) | 173 |
| Paula Gillen (11) | 174 |
| Lisa Cole (12) | 174 |
| Caitriona McKenna (12) | 175 |
| Dearbhla Cunningham (11) | 175 |

# The Poems

# Like A Student

Tell me a tale of the table,
I wanna learn some more.
Sing me a song of the wise old man
Who brings a briefcase through the door.

He offers you homework and questions
But you say, 'My schedule is full.'
Don't turn him a blind eye or make him mad,
You'll be lucky if you stick to the rule

And once upon a time in a classroom study hall
When my bag near put out my back, my strength
Was limited to two books or three
And the only one with four was me.
There's nothing left to do when your work is done
Just sit your ground and read your book, read your file
For the next day, for the next day will come.
Don't be worried cos the marking's done.

Give me a lecture on what's next to do,
What the poet has to say to you.
Just be careful when you mention all the golden rules,
Only one but your schedule is full.

But time is ticking and it's ticking fast
And my patience gone away, he's racing for the day
Like a man on a motor in the motor of a man
Safe and sound, coming round and he won't give way.
Little test, long computer passwords, fall off my seat.
I can see them in a mile but it's still not complete
For the next day, another new day will come
Don't be worried all your marking's done.

**Daniel Wray (18)**

# The Battle

The stadium erupts.
The giants enter the coliseum,
The fans ignore the amusements,
There's a war on over there.

The kicker starts the game,
The fans hold their breath in expectation,
All eyes on the players.
The war's started over here.

Ten minutes gone, no score.
Twenty minutes gone, still no score.
Thirty minutes gone, we're 3-0 down,
There's more than a war on over here.

Half-time comes,
The heads are down,
Fans drown their sorrows in their pints.
The war's starting again over here.

Ten minutes remain, it's three points all.
'Injury time,' says the ref.
Drop-goal attempt. It's there!
A war's been won over here!

**David Burke  (12)**

# Jack Frost

Jack Frost was in my garden,
I saw him there at dawn,
He was dancing round Mum's bushes,
And prancing on Dad's lawn.
He had a cloak that was silver,
A hat that shimmered white with glittering stardust,
And shoes that were shining and bright.

Jack Frost was in my garden,
And when I went out to play,
He nipped my fingers and toes,
And he quickly ran away.
I chased him round the shed,
And now I am sad to say,
Although I chased him everywhere,
He just would not stay.

Jack Frost was in my garden,
Now I would like to know,
Where can I find him hiding?
I've looked high and low.

**Rachel Stewart  (13)**


# A Sweet Face

Skin as soft as silk,
A head like a sunflower,
Eyes as bright as stars,
A nose like a button,
Cheeks as soft as peaches,
Lips the colour of cherries,
Teeth as white as snow.

**Stephanie Dowell  (13)**
**Antrim Grammar School**

# Talking

Talking, talking, talking,
That's all people ever do.
There are some who never stop,
And others who do.

It must feel quite upsetting,
To never talk at all.
To sit and think and wonder,
What life's purpose is for you.

Have you ever had these thoughts,
Like you wish that you were talking?
To tell your friends what you did at school,
And who you saw when you were walking.

As I was sitting in my house,
These thoughts came to my mind.
How lucky I am to talk and sing!
If only we could say nice things.

So, next time you feel like saying
Something cruel or mean.
Remember you've got a gift,
Don't waste it in on those words.

**Ruth Young (13)**
**Antrim Grammar School**


# Wintertime

I love wintertime when I snuggle up to a warm fire,
To hear the crispy sound of snow under a tyre,
Kids all wrapped up with hats, scarves and gloves
To build a snowman and have snowball fights, that's
what I really love.
When hearing the weather forecast, I wish for snow,
So that I can watch it glistening and enjoy its warm glow.

**Emma Hinfey (12)**
**Antrim Grammar School**

# Rugby

I hit a guy in the back,
My coach went *whack,*
The ref agreed with him
And I went to the sin bin.

When I got back on,
Everything went wrong.
My throws were on course,
But they tackled with a lot of force.

The half-time whistle blew,
We thought we were through,
I said, 'Send out Stu,'
But he came in two!

When the game ended,
Half our team needed mending.
So, we lost the game.

**Scott Stevenson (12)**
**Antrim Grammar School**


# The Black Horse Of The Dunes

He was as black as the night
And as fast as the wind.
His legs were like iron pistols
As he shot away in the night.
His muscles, rippling in the moonlight,
He ran over the dunes and through the valleys.
As tireless as the wind he raced,
His spirit was as wild as the woods.
No one could ever tame him,
He was here, there, everywhere.
And none could ever catch him,
He was the Black Horse of the Dunes.

**Anna-Claire McMahon (13)**
**Antrim Grammar School**

# It

It lives in a cupboard
Under the stairs,
I hear It yap all night.
It scares my little sister
And gives me such a fright.

My dad says It has
Eight eyes on stalks
Sticking out of its purple head.
I hear It creak and cry
When I have gone to bed.

It has ten legs,
Each leg has two feet.
It has pink and fuzzy hair
And I don't want to meet
This scary creature in its lair.

It eats fried worms
With pickled eggs
And mouldy old cheese.
All I want to say to It is
'Leave us alone . . .
*Please!'*

**Rachel Steele  (12)**
**Antrim Grammar School**

# Something

It's behind me
It's in front of me
It's in the air, it's everywhere
It's to my left
It's to my right
It's always out of sight
I can feel it close
It's something, but I just don't know what!

**Hannah Gourley  (13)**
**Antrim Grammar School**

# The Middle Class

When you're middle class,
You're sitting in-between,
You're not a wealthy millionaire,
But never in great need.

When your money grows on trees,
You can buy just anything,
From fancy clothes to flashy cars,
Or big rock diamond rings.

But when you're sitting in your mansion,
Feeling bored and all alone,
Sure, you've got the money,
But loneliness takes its toll.

It's the other side I really worry for,
Their hunger and their pain,
The homeless and malnourished,
Just pleading for the rain.

On the barren plains of Africa,
Working day and night,
Struggling every day of their lives.
Staying alive is the real fight.

Dirty water threatening death,
Expensive walls of glass,
I don't want to be any of these,
I'd rather be middle class.

**Ben Tisdale (13)**
**Antrim Grammar School**

# I Want . . .

I want to be famous
It is my dream,
Walking down the red carpet
With the cameras on me.

I want to earn lots of money
And act real cool,
Have a limo in the drive
And a massive indoor pool.

I want to wear designer clothes,
Gucci, Gap and Morgan,
Have pretty diamonds, rubies and rings,
Just some of my favourite things.

I want to have a butler,
A housekeeper and a cook,
A chauffeur and a gardener,
To fit in with my look.

I so want to be famous,
It is my dream,
For people to stand and stare,
Saying, 'Oh, isn't she supreme.'

**Rachel Surgenor  (12)**
**Antrim Grammar School**

# Budgie

B rilliantly flying all around my room,
U nder the table, over my head,
D own under my bed,
G liding smoothly to my sister's room,
I nto her make-up and her dolls,
E nraged she calls, 'Get this bird out!'

**Brent Esler  (12)**
**Antrim Grammar School**

# The Hockey Squad

Hammy-Jo jumps over the ball,
Emma Minford, glossing her lips,
Natalie and Bryony highlighting each other,
Stephanie, the pink Barbie,
Claire mastering the art of balancing on hockey balls,
Rachel carefully aims but sadly misses,
Pinky, that's me, a headless chicken playing golf,
Ruth Young, a dog following a bone,
Emma, do not be fooled by cute appearances,
Funny bones Hannah smiling away,
Leanne, a blonde ballerina,
Daroma, slaps the ball,
Catherine, don't hit it across the goals!
Brain being killed by the electric fences,
Ruth, turning and turning around and around,
Laura hitting other team members with her stick,
Rachel practising her hits with the ground,
Sarah-Jane who likes to run round the circle,
Miss McKee our trusty team coach, who can be heard all
over the field shouting, 'Welly it, welly it!'

No one is perfect. This is my squad, we try our best to beat the odds!

**Amy Duncan (13)**
Antrim Grammar School


# A Day To Remember

A day to remember, racing my dad,
In a go-kart in Cornwall, both quite mad.
Wheel to wheel battle; Mum watching in fear.
Me and my dad, both driving in top gear.
The chequered flag near the finish in sight,
I am the winner of this brilliant fight.
The race is now over, Mum is so glad!
Poor Dad licks his wounds, defeat is so sad.

**Michael Duncan (13)**
Antrim Grammar School

# Death . . .

I wonder when it's going to hit
Could it be now or then?
Who knows? I don't, do you?
I wish I did know, then I could be prepared
I take it day by day, wondering all the time
Worrying at every noise
Even though I know it wasn't it.
Trying not to worry makes it even worse,
Looking over my shoulder every minute of every day.
People always think I'm crazy
Puzzled over this one thing that might not happen for
Years to come
But one thing's for sure
When it comes, I will be ready . . .

**Stephanie Houston (12)**
**Antrim Grammar School**


# The Land 'If Only'

People drive themselves crazy,
    In the land of 'If Only'.

'If only I hadn't done this,
    If only I had done that,'
    Is all you hear them say.

If you keep yourself in the land of 'If Only'
    You'll be there all the time.

'If only I hadn't done this,
    If only I had done that,'
    Is all you hear them say.

People drive themselves crazy,
    In the land of 'If Only'.

**Joanna Hamilton (12)**
**Antrim Grammar School**

# This Time Of Year

Open the door to go for a walk,
The cold air is a surprise!
Suddenly the summer has gone,
How quickly the year flies!

The air is sharp, the sky is dark
And the streets are quiet and still,
But we feel great comfort in our warm clothes
And think that this is brill!

Because the weather tells us
That Christmas will soon be here,
The decorations, the presents, excitement,
It is drawing near!

So what if it is cold,
Or there is a drop of rain,
Christmas will see us through
'Til spring comes again!

**Louise Glover  (12)**
**Antrim Grammar School**


# Midnight

In the chilly hour of midnight, spirits come alive.
In the chilly hour of midnight,
wolf cubs thrive.
In the chilly hour of midnight, darkness
fills the land.
In the chilly hour of midnight, nothing is bland.
In the chilly hour of midnight,
owls stalk wary prey.
In the chilly hour of midnight,
the sun eagerly anticipates the day.
In the chilly hour of midnight, the moon's light
lies across the ground.
In the chilly hour of midnight, there is no one
to be found.

**Cassie Dawson  (12)**
**Antrim Grammar School**

# Winter

Winter's cold, winter's harsh to people and to animals both,
Winter's cold, winter's harsh.

Winter's dark, winter's windy that blows down trees and causes
accidents,
Winter's dark, winter's windy.
Winter's snowy, winter's slippery on roads at night and pavements
white,
Winter's snowy, winter's slippery.

Winter's gloomy, winter's wet, dripping trees and puddled roads,
Winter's gloomy, winter's wet.

Glowing fires and hot soup keeps away winter's cold.

Snowball fights and snowmen, make winter good fun.

Christmas lights and presents chase away winter's dark day.

Wellington boots and warm coats help deal with winter's wet.

**Lee Dougan (12)**
**Antrim Grammar School**


# Life!

Why live a life of boredom?
Why live a life of pain?
Why live a life of unhappiness?
Why live a live of shame?

Some people ignore their life of boredom,
Ignore their life of pain,
Ignore their life of unhappiness,
Ignore their life of shame.

I want a life with no boredom,
A life without the pain,
A life of only happiness,
A life free from shame.

**Kirsty Fleming (13)**
**Antrim Grammar School**

# Rainbow

After a rainstorm you suddenly appear
I am so glad that you are here
Above the clouds your eyes do peer
Or in the sky so clear
I will always love to see you glimmer
When you travel near
I will always greet you with a friendly cheer!

In the warm or in the cold
There is always a story to be told
About the rainbow so bright and bold.

The first time it was seen in history
Your appearance, it was a mystery
Until the rains stopped that day
For our sins we had to pay
Then you appeared from
Heaven above, to remind us
Of God's love.

**Rachel Ingram  (12)**
**Antrim Grammar School**


# Hallowe'en

The end of October is nearly in sight,
It is the best time for having a fright.

Vampires and ghosts who you would not like to greet,
Children knocking on doors asking trick or treat.

Fireworks and sparklers go off with a spark,
While pumpkins and candles glow in the dark.

We all sit around the bonfire to keep warm,
As the bats fly away in a swarm.

Witches and ghouls and headless ghosts,
At Hallowe'en these are all our hosts,
That is why I love it the most.

**Sarah Dennison  (12)**
**Antrim Grammar School**

# My Genie Friend

I used to have a friend
Almost anything he could mend
He was a genie like the one in the story
He was called Rory.

As you would know
Three wishes I could throw
The first was spent on a dog
Until it ran after a frog.

The second wish I thought carefully
And often sometimes to prayerfully
I decided in the end
To wish for a new life.

The life was luxury
With many cool parties
But everything was so boring
I ended up snoring.

That wish was my very last
I dreamt of my past
I asked for my old life back
I had had enough of wishes!

**Hannah Hamilton  (11)**
**Antrim Grammar School**


# Slumberland

Here in my world where there is only me,
I can set all my problems and feelings free,
I'm relaxed and happy, joyful and sad,
I'm somewhere no one can hurt me,
Or make me mad.
It's my world.
In the background there plays a band.
It's my world, it's Slumberland.

**Rachel Herod  (12)**
**Antrim Grammar School**

# A Snowman

I was born a snowflake
Which was white and awake.
My eyes and buttons are pieces of coal
My scarf is red and my hat is a bowl.

At night when the stars come out
I come alive and walk about.
And greet the animals that come out at night
But then the moon disappears from sight.

The sun begins to come out
All the birds were flying about.
Morning began to break
But I have a terrible ache.

The buttons were sliding down my tummy
Then I cried for my mummy.
The hat I wore fell off my head
And in the end I was dead.

**Atholl Easton (11)**
**Antrim Grammar School**


# Why War?

Why did some men hate so much that they were prepared to die?
To bring terror to America from a clear September sky.
America was wounded and desperate for a plan,
Their leader shouted loud and clear, 'We'll bomb Afghanistan,
The country's full of terrorists and men of cruel heart,
Our B52s will avenge us and blow them all apart!'
The war was over quickly, not content with this small gain.
They bombed Iraq into the Stone Age and deposed Saddam Hussein.
The civilians suffered most of all, a proud and noble race.
To be crushed and occupied by invaders, the ultimate disgrace.
A father buries his family under a scorching desert sky.
Why do some men hate so much that they are prepared to die?

**Anna Elliott (12)**
**Antrim Grammar School**

# Silence

She was walking and there was silence,
Not a person in her sight,
She walked through the empty, deserted village,
Without a worry in the world.

Lonely now,
She wanders on,
The eerie silence falls around her,
She wishes she were back at home,
Where her radio blasts a constant beat.

Then all at once she hears it,
A dull and rhythmic thud.
Puzzled, she stops and listens
And realises why.
There's never really silence,
If you listen for the beat of your heart.

**Nicola McCleery  (11)**
**Antrim Grammar School**


# My World

My world is full of books,
People who don't care about looks.

My world is a cinema screen,
Theme park rides that don't make me scream.

My world is full of trees,
Fields, flowers and honeybees.

My world is a place,
Where there is peace among the human race.

My world is with my family, my friends
And my animals.

My world is my house,
My home.

**Lucy Finn  (12)**
**Antrim Grammar School**

# The Alphabet

A is for Alex, who eats apples every day
B is for Bobby, who boogies to da beat
C is for Chloe, who chew chocolate
D is for Dora, who loves dogs
E is for Ellie the elephant, who lost her trunk
F is for Freddy, who loves frogs
G is for Gail, who talks to goats
H is for Harry, who races horses
I is for Ingrid, who lives in an igloo
J is for John, who jumps
K is for kind Kerry, who helps everyone
L is for Laura, who loves Louis
M is for Mary, who makes money
N is for Nichola, who names Normans
O is for Opal, which is a very famous stone
P is for Peter, who pats parrots
Q is for Queen Q
R is for Rudolph and his big red nose
S is for snow with which we have snowball fights
T is for Terry, who talks to trees
U is for unicorns and their big horns
V is for Victoria, who is always victorious
W is for Wilma, who loves walking
X is for X-rays of skeletons
Y is for yoghurt that splats everywhere
Z is for zebras that are black and white.

**Victoria Harvey (11)**
**Antrim Grammar School**


# My Dream

Moonlight glistening across a wonderful lake
Fairies dancing who don't make mistakes
Rose petals swirling in the gentle breeze
And butterflies fluttering past wondrous trees
This is my world, I don't want to leave it
But it's only a dream - too bad I can't live it.

**Yvonne Field (12)**
**Antrim Grammar School**

# What's For Tea?

Do I want an Indian
Or will we get Chinese?
Mum might send for a pizza
With tomato, ham and cheese.

What about lasagne
Or spaghetti Bolognese?
I like Caesar salad,
With a blob of mayonnaise.

Now my sister is a veggie,
So we can't have sirloin steak
And I don't want a carrot stick,
Even for my health's sake.

We could go to the chippy,
For old-fashioned fish and chips,
Then we'd have a problem,
When the fat goes on our hips.

'Oh hurry up and make your choice,
What is it you want most?'
'I know Mum, I've sorted it.
I'd just like *beans on toast!'*

**Jayne McGlaughlin  (11)**
Antrim Grammar School

# Thunderstorm

Animals stumble as fright turns to flight
Tall trees crumble with a crash
In terror the hound will dash
As forks flash across the dark night.

Silvery shivers travel through my spine
As crashing clouds rumble
And rain lashes at such a pace
Many make haste to a faraway place.

**Gillian Fleming  (12)**
Antrim Grammar School

# The Squirrel

I like squirrels, red and grey,
They sleep at night and work all day.
So listen up, you ought to know,
How the greys make the little reds go.

The little reds eat fruit and nuts,
While the greys drive them nuts.
The native reds are in danger,
While the greys charm the rangers.

The poor little reds, they're dying out,
Why don't the greys get thrown out?
Who agrees that something needs to be done?
Take the greys back to their native home.

Well, well, well, what do you know?
Time is up, I have to go.
So now you know about the reds and greys,
How they sleep all night and work all day.

**Nicola McKee (11)**
**Antrim Grammar School**

# Raindrops

Raindrops on my window
And on the rooftops too
It seems as though it will not end
As the sky is grey not blue.

I hear the raindrops tumbling
On the treetops high
The rain is getting on my nerves
So I heave a weary sigh.

The rain is getting heavier
The rain is getting loud
The sun is not shining
I can see it's not proud.

**Shana Irvine (12)**
**Antrim Grammar School**

# A Dangerous Game

Swooping softly through the night,
Hunting with eyes so gleaming bright,
For a movement in the shadowy trees.
But, in the carpet of forest leaves,
There stirred a mouse,
From its leafy house.
It softly crept along the ground,
With hardly any sound.
Slinking softly through the leaves
And underneath the shadowy trees.

The owl, hunting for its prey,
Saw the mouse creep swiftly away,
It dived so quickly from the sky
And kept its bright, unblinking eyes,
Upon the mouse as along it ran,
Running as quickly as a mouse can,
Trying to escape from being prey,
Wanting to live to the next day.
The mouse ran inside a hollow log
And silently came a murky fog.
The owl's hunt ended, oh so quickly
And home it flew to its hollow tree.

The mouse learned a lesson the difficult way
And lived to see another day!

**Rachel Lewis (11)**
**Antrim Grammar School**


# What Am I?

The cold, fast-flowing substance,
Can be blue, green or white.
It swirls in its storms
And is calm at night.
It supplies lots of food
And we swim in it too.
What am I? Have a guess, please do!

**Calum McGill (11)**
**Antrim Grammar School**

# Daddy Don't Go

Daddy why are you shouting?
You're making me cry,
You're packing your bags and leaving me behind . . .

Daddy, don't cry,
Daddy, don't go,
Daddy don't say goodbye . . .

I don't want to lose you
You don't want to lose me
But if you leave now will I have lost you?

Daddy, you're not listening,
You're starting to walk out,
Daddy don't make me scream and shout
Daddy, I love you
Daddy, don't you love me too?

Please Daddy don't cry
Please Daddy don't go
Please Daddy remember I tried
But I guess now's the time to say goodbye.

**Jade Mackey (11)**
**Antrim Grammar School**


# Magic Flute

I saw a scary witch last night,
She swooped down low and gave me a fright.
I tried to run as fast as I could,
But she was quick and in a bad mood.
She cried out, 'Just for you, I'll cast a spell,
At the count of three, like a skunk you'll smell!'
What she didn't know was that I was cute,
I began to play on my magic flute.
When she heard this, she flew away
And I smelt great for another day!

**Louise McBride (11)**
**Antrim Grammar School**

# Dreamland

Each hour, each day, I can't concentrate
Longing for it to come
For the end of the day
When the sun goes to sleep
And rests till another dawn.

I long to lay down my weary head
And dream of non-existent things
Like dragons, fairies and cars that can fly
Along with all the happy hours sleep brings.

It's a time when we don't worry
When all misery disappears
And problems seem to go away
For years and years and years.

But when the time comes
To drift off into sleep
Happy thoughts come with us all the way
They fill us with glee
On the inside and out
And when our mothers check on us we have nothing to say.

We have now entered the merriest world -
*Dreamland.*

**Amy McIlwaine  (11)**
**Antrim Grammar School**

# Migration

The birds fly away slowly,
Into the gloom,
A man stands there, watching,
He knows they won't return soon.

The man sits and waits,
As the last bird flies away
And with a sigh, he stands up and says,
'Another day, friend, another day.'

**Emma McFadden  (11)**
**Antrim Grammar School**

# The Greatest Fear

Monsters and demons with pointy teeth,
All kinds of snakes beyond belief,
Crocodiles, rhinos and grizzly bears,
All of these things would give him a scare.

Witches and warlocks with big, long wands,
Heights, cliff edges and very deep ponds,
Lorries, trucks and extinguished light,
All of these things would give him a fright.

Pirates, werewolves and rickety stairs,
Ghosts and ghouls and scary nightmares,
Bees, wasps and loud noises from near,
All of these are things that he fears.

Now that he's older he sees these were daft,
He now looks back and does nothing but laugh,
He no longer fears things that lurk,
The only thing he fears, is piles of *homework!*

**Mark James Lewis (11)**
**Antrim Grammar School**

# Teddy

Teddy, Teddy, where are you?
I just don't know what I'd do without you.
Your fur so soft and your black, chestnut eyes.
When I first saw you it really was a surprise.
But now I'm sad to say goodbye,
I knew this would happen some day,
Not knowing why!
But I've grown old and grown out of teddy bears,
So I'm giving you now to someone who cares
And who also loves teddy bears.
*Goodbye!*

**Natalie McCabe (11)**
**Antrim Grammar School**

# Lessons

I'm sitting in a lesson
Bored to tears
Listening to the teacher talk -
Suddenly, I'm in a world of galloping deers,
Weird or what?

The streets are made of chocolate,
I race forward happily,
The chocolate tastes delicious,
This is way better than reality.

Everything's getting fuzzy,
My world is fading fast,
A voice breaks the silence,
'No homework class,'
I can't believe it.

*Weird or what?*

**Karen McKnight (12)**
**Antrim Grammar School**


# School

Moving schools, brand new rules,
Losing friends, finding new ones.
Brand new lessons, some old ones too,
Losing your way in a big, new school.
Lots more teachers and assembly,
Starting school early, coming home late.
Heavy schoolbag, lots more books,
More time for homework, less time for fun.
Hot school dinners, tasty for some.
Walking to the station, waiting for the bus to come.
Five more years to come, looks like great fun.

**Lauren Milligan (11)**
**Antrim Grammar School**

# The Creepiness Of The Night!

The darkness,
The coldness,
The creepiness of the night!

You sit at home,
With nothing but fear,
The creepiness of the night!

The time has come,
You're all alone,
The creepiness of the night!

You fall asleep,
They're gone,
The fears have gone!

You wake up,
The day goes by
And there's not a cloud in the sky!

It's time for bed!
*Oh no, not again!*

The creepiness of the night!

**Rebecca McAllister (11)**
**Antrim Grammar School**


# Black And White Fur

Black and white fur, running through the trees,
Black and white fur, I wonder what he sees?
Could it be a bird or even a mouse?
Or is it just that he's wanting to go in my house?
Black and white fur, off he goes at speed,
Black and white fur, pays no heed.
Black and white fur, you're really very smart,
Black and white fur, with you I will not part.
Black and white fur, belongs to my cat,
Black and white fur, is now sleeping on the mat!

**Genna McGilton (12)**
**Antrim Grammar School**

# Poem About Homework

Homework is the dreaded word,
I'm sure you will agree.
A word I wish I'd never heard,
I'm sick of it, you see.

'This is your homework for next day,'
Is all I ever hear.
That's what teachers always say,
Giving you a satisfied sneer.

They think it's all right to give us
Twenty lots of homework a day.
To them they think it's no big fuss,
In a grown-up way.

It tears away our weekend,
Unless we get it done.
But thinking just around the bend,
Another homework week will have just begun.

**Scott Newton  (12)**
**Antrim Grammar School**

# The Mysterious One

In all of my life so solemn and true;
I have never once met you.
Your eyes so bright they could light up the sky,
Your lips so smooth, never let out a sigh.
None of my dreams have ever come true
Although it might seem that I've seen you.
On a misty night all the birds have gone,
I think, I think I hear a song.
And although I cannot see anyone,
I know you are there, the mysterious one.

**Carrie McClenaghan  (11)**
**Antrim Grammar School**

# When I Look

When I look into the sky
I always really wonder why
Why the stars shine so bright
And why they only come out at night.

When I look and see the planets
I wish I could be there someday
But these are only hopes and dreams
Because planets are so far away.

When I look and see the moon
Shining like a big balloon
In the dark sky, big and bright
It really is a beautiful sight.

When I look and see the sun
I get excited, it's time for fun
The sandy beach is not so far
Let's get ready, get in the car.

A happy, funfilled day ahead
When it's done, it's time for bed
A tired mind, it's time for sleep
Precious memories I will always keep.

**Chloé-Jade McDonald (11)**
**Antrim Grammar School**

# Sea Calm, Sea Rage

I am the sea and calm I am.
My job's to be calm and soothing
And give these people life,
But I get angry too.
I can destroy whole cities
With one swipe of my arms.
Make volcanoes, earthquakes and more
And destroy the Earth as we know it,
Although, I choose *not* to,
I just rest under the sun.

**Pearse McCoy (11)**
Antrim Grammar School

# Destiny

Look at the chestnut beauty,
The care she has for her young,
The loving and caring old pony,
Lives in a field of dung.

All day she stands by the barn,
On a lonely patch of green,
Not a sinner in sight of the farm,
Just Tess and the foal to be seen.

From a distance, someone has spied her,
Looking so lonely and sad,
At last someone has found her,
No more the need to be sad.

The horse and its kin are free now,
Away from a life of neglect,
Gone to fresh fields of pasture,
A happy, new life and respect.

**Toni Reid  (12)**
**Antrim Grammar School**


# Summer Holidays

I enjoyed the summer holidays,
spending time with all my mates,
instead of doing geography
and studying all the states.

Going to the Antrim Forum
and swimming in the pool,
taking our minds off doing work
and starting back to school.

Lazy, sunny, summer days,
lying in bed till noon,
making the best of no work at school
as the new term comes too soon.

**Walter Todd  (11)**
**Antrim Grammar School**

# My Cat, Dora

I've a cat called Dora
Her fur is black and white
She sleeps during the day
And goes out during the night.

My cat eats Whiskas
And drinks lots of milk
And when I stroke her
It feels like silk.

She loves to climb trees
And has a friend called Pickles
They like to chase leaves
And they loved to be tickled.

When I come home
She starts to purr
My little cat Dora
I really love her.

**Olivia Telford  (11)**
**Antrim Grammar School**


# Tree

Tree, tree so high,
With your branches touching the sky
You're always growing
Your age is never showing
You've blossomed, withered, yet never died
Has anyone ever explained to you why?
Your leaves are green, brown and red
And some of them appear dead
In winter your branches are quite bare
Your leaves have vanished, do you know where?
Your trunk says that you are old
Though I see no death, moss or mould
When we see you once again
You'll look like something near the beginning, not the end.

**Rachael Whyte  (11)**
**Antrim Grammar School**

# Basil The Bulldog

We have a white bulldog called Basil
He is as fat as a pot-bellied pig
When he tries to get on the sofa
He can't, cos his belly's too big

I really love my fat bulldog
He is the best friend I've ever had
With his bandy legs and wrinkled-up face
He's the spitting image of my dad

When I say to my dog, 'Let's go walkies,'
He goes hyper and runs round the place
Basil ends up taking me walkies
I usually end up flat on my face

When it's time for us all to retire
And Basil is tucked up in bed
His sleep is so deep, his snoring's so loud
It's enough to waken the dead.

**Scott Thompson (11)**
**Antrim Grammar School**


# I Had!

I had a coat made of wool,
Which my brothers changed for an old stool.
I had a top that had spots,
Which my brothers tied in knots.
I had some lovely gold laces,
Which my brothers exchanged for worn braces.
I had a little beige bag,
Which my brothers swapped for a stag.
I had a lot of stuff,
Which my brothers destroyed for their fluff.
I had a lovely room,
Which is now my biggest doom.

**Elspeth Jean Woolsey (12)**
**Antrim Grammar School**

# The Wonderful Seasons

Life begins in springtime, the beginning of the year,
The lambs they gambol in the field,
The snowdrops they appear,
The feel-good factor's all around, affecting how we feel.

Summertime's my favourite,
The holidays, you know.
Those carefree days of pleasure,
In the sunshine, all aglow.

Autumn, when our birds migrate
And some animals get ready to hibernate,
Leaves, they die and change their colours,
Reds and yellows and many others.

Winter, when the breezes blow,
Bringing rain and lots of snow,
Short days, long nights,
To sit before the fire bright.

**Rebecca Simpson (12)**
**Antrim Grammar School**


# Fear

Fear is a blunt knife stabbing my back.
Fear is dark, almost black.
It stands my hairs up on end
And is very hard to bend.

Fear is like drowning in the sea
Or a monster chasing me.
It sounds like constant shattering glass.
People hope the fear will pass.

Fear is not as bright as gold.
Fear is very far from bold.
Fear is nowhere, far nor near.
Fear. Fear. Fear.

**Stephen Campbell (12)**
**Antrim Grammar School**

# My Fear!

My fear was her dying.
My nana dying.
Why did she have to die?

My fear was life without her.
Why couldn't she have lived for another few years?
Why did she have to die?

My fear was her leaving me to face the world alone.
She was always there, but now she's not.
Why did she have to die?

My fear was never seeing her again.
But life has to go on.
Why did she have to die?

She was my nana and I loved her.
I always have loved her and I will never stop.
I didn't want her to die but she did.
At least I know she is away to a better place than I am.
Glad that I don't have to watch her suffer any longer.
But why did she have to leave me?
She always said I could get where I wanted in life
And I am going to do that for her.
She may have left my life, but she will never leave my heart!

**Michelle Carnwath (12)**
**Antrim Grammar School**


# Fear Is . . .

Fear tastes like a bitter lemon,
it smells like a musty, old house,
it feels like being afraid and worried,
it looks like a dying dog
and reminds me of being bullied,
*again!*

**Jamie David Blair (13)**
**Antrim Grammar School**

# Daughter's Grief

I see fear in your eyes
As you try to tell me.
I hear fear in your voice
As it quivers.

What could be so bad?
I just don't know.
Do I really want to hear
Your words of woe?

No, I don't believe you,
No, I don't want to know.
Please don't say it
Don't let it be so.

Now you have gone
I know what you said to be true
I didn't want to believe it
But death has shown it to be true.

Now there is fear in my eyes,
As I look for you.
And fear in my voice,
As I grieve for you.

**Leeanne Allen  (13)**
**Antrim Grammar School**


# Principal's Detention

The fear of a principal's detention,
Maybe seems like fun to some,
But it's obviously quite a bum,
Having to get up on a Saturday,
Just like Monday had already come,
For those three hours all you do is sit
And think, what have I done?
The thought of a principal's DT,
Is enough to put the fear in me!

**Jonathan Beers  (12)**
**Antrim Grammar School**

# Courage

I know I have it,
I just can't find it,
My mum says I've got it,
But where did I put it?

I'll tell you where I put it,
Because I've just found it,
It's hidden deep down inside me,
But it has just leaped out.

It happened today,
When my friend was being bullied,
I was the one who helped her,
I did my best to protect her.

I told those bullies to leave her alone,
I told them I would tell,
They called me names but I didn't care,
Because good old courage helped me out there.

**Eve Cairns (12)**
**Antrim Grammar School**


# Boo!

On Hallowe'en night, I was in the haunted house on my own,
It was dark in the house; the electric had fused,
All you could hear was the chime of a clock, as it struck midnight.
Suddenly, a door banged!
It was as loud as a kodo drummer.
I shook under my sheets, like a timid mouse hiding from a cat,
The lion of a wind roaring through the cracks in the walls and windows.
When morning came, my fear was gone,
But only for a little while.
I went slowly downstairs and approached the front door,
When a spider landed on my shoulder and whispered, 'Boo!'
I screamed like a banshee and ran out the door,
The spider turned and asked, 'Was it something I said?'

**Kirsty Barr (12)**
**Antrim Grammar School**

# But Why?

We're supposed to be better off now than we used to be,
Now that we have the money to put men on the moon and explore
                                                        space,
But why is world hunger still an issue?

We're supposed to be better off now than we used to be,
What with all our 'weapons of mass destruction',
But why aren't the nations at peace?

We're supposed to be better off than we used to be,
Now that we have better technology and more scientists,
But why are people still dying of cancer?

We're supposed to be better off now than we used to be,
With many different technological advances,
But are we really?

We're supposed to be better off now than we used to be,
I think that until we have an end to world hunger, peace and cures
                to life-threatening diseases (or at least some of them),
That we're not!

**Catherine Arrell  (12)**
Antrim Grammar School


# Alone

I have been alone all my life,
24/7 I am alone,
Nobody knows me,
Nobody likes me.
I feel like I am endlessly drifting in space
Darker and deeper into nothingness.
When I die nobody will miss me,
Nobody will cry for me,
I will always be alone.

**Reece Campbell  (12)**
Antrim Grammar School

# Black

I stand alone in the corner,
Waiting for daylight to shine.
People may think I'm a mourner,
Because of these black clothes of mine.
Taxis rumble past and ignore me,
Am I standing in the wrong place?
Or then again, could it be,
They rumble on by when they see my colour or my race?
It sickens me to think of the world,
As a cold and prejudiced place.
And all the times my stomach has curled,
When people jeer at the colour of my face.
I stand alone in the corner,
Waiting for daylight to shine.
People may think I'm a mourner,
Because of these black clothes of mine.

**Claire Adams (12)**
**Antrim Grammar School**

# Do I Get Any Gratitude?

I, the fireman, have to risk my life each day for *you!*
Do I get any gratitude? Yes.
My heart, as brave as a lion's.
I run into blazing houses to save babies from sure death!
Do I get any gratitude? Yes.
Like a gallant horse I run, straight through the flames
To rescue the elderly!
Do I get any gratitude? Yes.

The bell is ringing.
It's time to go.
Now I must put on my brave show!

**Benjamin Cathcart (12)**
**Antrim Grammar School**

# Depression And Pain

I feel so lonely,
The depression is clear,
It's feeding on my fears.
I fear the darkness taking over me,
I need someone to come and set me free,
It binds me to this world.

The pain's killing me,
It's just too much to bear,
I just want to fade into the night
And with that everyone would just forget me.
I could just end my life
And the pain would just disappear.

**Jan Parkhill  (14)**
**Antrim Grammar School**


# Me, Mouse

Me, Mouse
I live in my house,
But the cat lives outside
So all I do is hide.
If I go out I get eaten
Or maybe I might get beaten,
I'm so scared in here
I'm full of fear.
My hole in the wall
Is very, very small.
Me, Mouse
I live in my house
Down the Appletree Road.

**Lyndsey-Anne Coulter  (12)**
**Antrim Grammar School**

# Ghosts

To most, ghosts are just a tale,
    Known to fly and float and sail.
To some children they are just a game,
    Some ghosts have a funny name.
Casper, Stinky, Stretch and Fatty,
    These four ghosts would drive you batty.
But some are not from a book,
    You may just see one if you stop and look.
These strange things don't use a door
    They come through walls and do even more!
There's been so many stories of ghostly fun,
    If you put them together they'd weigh a ton.

**Michael Rutledge (12)**
**Antrim Grammar School**

# Forgotten Soldiers

The sun rose slowly,
Blazing overhead.
It illuminated young faces,
All of whom were dead.

Men gave up their lives
To die in a foreign land.
No time to say goodbye,
To hold a loved one's hand.

The battlefield, many years deserted,
No remnants of war.
Yet those worst affected
Will remember evermore.

**Caroline Hull (13)**
**Antrim Grammar School**

# Who Am I?

Who am I?
I am me.
I am from a culture
So well known.
A culture with a language
Which seems so strange,
Yet so cool
To those unknown to it.

A race with weird-shaped eyes,
Jet-black hair and tanned skin.
Can you guess who I am?
There are famous people
Who are from the same country.
People so famous,
If you truly realised that
You wouldn't make fun of them.

Do you know who I am?
A culture which should be treated,
Treated as equal as others.
A culture with the same dreams
And hopes as others.
A race who wants no prejudice,
A race who wants equality.
Have you guessed who I am?
I am a Chinese person.

**Tina Ho  (14)**
**Antrim Grammar School**

# Life On Mars

Mars is a planet, round and red,
Red like the sun only barren and dead.
Craters abound, lonely but free,
One stands watching, dark as could be.

Probes are going there, hoping to find
Life on Mars, an intelligent mind.
Creatures could live there, creatures could grow,
They could be friendly, they could be foe.

As you look out your window, lying in bed,
You see Mars as a red star, floating overhead.
We could be living there, once our planet has died,
So look up to your new home, a planet in the sky.

**Colin Hill (13)**
**Antrim Grammar School**


# Rugby

Like gladiators in Rome,
Standing tall and strong.
When the whistle blows
They charge to kill.
Feel their mighty wrath!
Try after try goes over,
Kick after kick goes through,
In scrums *no mercy*,
In lineouts no prisoners.
My heroes stand
Dressed in green -
Ireland.

**Ashley McClenaghan (14)**
**Antrim Grammar School**

# Black As Night

Her voice gave great meaning
As it floated softly on the gentle breeze.
Too bad,
It was as if
She was talking to a solid brick wall,
All because she had skin as black as night,
Talking to a snow-white man.

He held his nose aloft
As she tried to get through,
To no avail.
His ears were blocked,
Through and through.
His nose shone as the sun glinted off it,
Pointed upwards towards the sky.

She kept her head held high,
It did not fall in shame.
The treatment she got
Because of her skin,
Was always the same
From the white,
Whose nose was in the air.

**Cherith Hamilton (13)**
**Antrim Grammar School**


# Violence

Is violence the answer? Maybe in some cases, maybe not.
However, not the first suggestion to solving a problem.
Think.
Just think of the consequences that will arise,
Once you resort to violence.
Maybe if you are violent towards someone
They will be violent back, but do you really want to be in bother?
I thought not! So, please stop the violence.
Every action has a reaction.

**Haseeb Gulzar (13)**
**Antrim Grammar School**

# From A 22nd Century Window

Moving along, fast as light
Speeding round a site,
I see the Millennium Dome
Built way before I was born.
Then go up into the sky,
There's my home way up high.
Flying right down into the sea,
Cities, homes, lots to see.
Not very many fish to see,
It's all just water and cities.
Go up high again, not to be rude,
But to see where Neil Armstrong stood.
Then I went to Mars,
There were Martians drinking, obviously at the bars.
Went back to Earth and thought,
*What happened since my great uncle Michael was born?*
A lot has changed, it will never be the same
Until the fat lady blows her horn.

**Michael Donnelly  (13)**
**Antrim Grammar School**

# Colourful Rain

Twisting, twirling, turning, swirling,
Caught up in their merry dance,
Intricate patterns, colours blending,
Children watching in a trance.

Buttery yellows, coppers, reds,
Colourful rain from the trees around,
Falling, falling, landing softly,
Silently blanketing the frosted ground.

Kicking Wellingtons, crunchy noises,
Children jumping in and out,
Laughter, fun and rosy faces,
Leaves are scattered all about.

**Rachael Hunter  (14)**
**Antrim Grammar School**

# The Seasons

S ummer, hot and very sunny,
U sing suncream, getting burnt isn't funny,
M aking sandcastles on the beach,
M eeting up with friends, no school for nine weeks,
E ating ice creams and cold iced drinks,
R ed skies mean lots of late nights.

A utumn leaves of golden colours can be found,
U sing them to jump and play on the ground,
T he acorns and nuts fall,
U sing conkers for fun in the playground,
M aking pots of money raking in leaves of gold,
N ot long until winter, it's starting to get cold.

W intertime has a lot of snow,
I can't wait till Christmas, presents, holly and mistletoe,
N ights are long and cold,
T he cold air freezes my breath,
E veryone wrapping up in woolly hats,
R ubbing their hands to keep warm.

S ometimes warm, sometimes cold,
P lenty of daffodils are sold,
R ainfall is likely but there's a spring in my step,
I nto the world come
N ewborn lambs, jumping around on the
G reen grass and green leaves that have grown.

**Alex Scott (14)**
**Ballyclare High School**

# Ballyclare High

B ell goes off, it's time for school,
A pen to write, this is my tool.
L ate for school, better hurry,
L ittle first years scuttle and scurry.
Y et again another day,
C afeteria, I'll never pay.
L ooking for homework, I'm being sincere,
A fter all it should be here.
R eady to learn, how hard can it be?
E very day is a year, do you agree?

H ere comes lunch, time for a treat,
I f only I had longer to eat.
G oing home, I can't wait,
H oping the bus isn't late!

**James Smyth (14)**
**Ballyclare High School**

# October

October arrived today,
A nip in the air, we say.
Winter takes a first grip,
On the ground we will slip.
The autumn flowers fade,
The bird-feeders, the robin will raid.
Swifts can be seen overhead,
The far north wind, we will soon dread.
All the leaves turn red, yellow and gold,
The weather turns suddenly cold.
To find the berries the animals must roam,
The best place for us is home.

**Christopher Williamson (12)**
**Ballyclare High School**

# The Vengeful Dragon

Hope is home and the heart is free.
A dragon's soul, the last on Earth,
Soars to find what can make the peace,
That he has sought for since his birth.

That dragon, Kurast, had one dying wish,
That he seek the vengeance for his mother.
So he was trapped to this world
Until he finds the love, destroyed.

Hope is home and the heart is free.
The days go by, some slow, some fast,
Reminding him of his lonely sorrow.
All he can do is remember the past.
He wonders, is there any rest for the wicked?

He roams to look for the source of his heartache,
All Kurast can do is remember
The awful scenes that he had to watch,
Of the Slayer taking his mother's life.
Just watching caused him all this stress and strife.

Kurast can tell that the end is near,
He fights and kills the Slayer.
He's very brave; he shows no fear,
To pay respect to the lives of those taken.

Hope is home and the heart is free.
Now he can rest in peace,
His vengeance now settled,
He wonders, who else lost family at an early age?

**Lauren Foster (15)**
**Ballyclare High School**

# The Building

When sitting on the bench, I gaze across the road
Eyeing up my enemy, for at the same time
I would find myself always sitting on that same bench day after day,
Gazing lovingly across that road, forever fixated at that one feature,
Never taking my eyes off it, never taking my eyes off my enemy.

Once we were friends but how I despise it,
Its very presence denied by my hatred.
This hatred, this pain would never die for my enemy
Was . . . a building, an insignificant terrace shop,
A monstrosity, a DIY shop.

It was not what this shop is but what it was once before,
For, before it was a part of my soul,
A boy's necessity, a sweet shop.
An innocent building, as innocent as the kind shopkeepers
                                                        who owned it.

Before that building across the road mutated into a place full of
Uninteresting products and services was once a building
Jam-packed with delicious delights that could tantalise the senses.
A shop of this calibre was unmatched, the best in the business.
Once it had gone, nothing mattered anymore.
A part of myself had been ripped away from me forever.

**Alan Finlay  (14)**
**Ballyclare High School**


# Friends

A friend is something who is there for you,
They'd make you feel better when you're feeling blue.
They'd be there for the happy times, and there for the sad.
You'd always appreciate them and always be glad.

You'll grow together, ride through thick and thin,
And if you're true you'll sail right through.
You'll always trust and depend,
Always look up to and respect a friend.

**Rebecca Hamilton  (13)**
**Ballyclare High School**

# The Terror That Hit Downtown

Tuesday morning had only begun,
Children were ready to have some fun.
Parents were already at work
Not knowing they were gonna be attacked by jerks!

They typed and printed and then
At dead on 8.46pm
The first plane hit Twin Tower one,
All the people could do was run.

Many people jumped, not knowing what to do,
They couldn't wait for the firefighter's crew.
Many had already lost sisters and brothers,
Many had lost fathers and mothers.

Three minutes later scared people below
Saw plane two hit tower two, hijacked by evil foes.
Not long after, tower one fell to the ground,
Then tower two fell into a debris mound.

Firefighters worked hard at their best
To try and find those who were at rest.
Many had died amongst the dirt and rubble,
Causing deaths to nearly double.

Many helped to dig for the dead.
Hours went on, nothing was said.
They worked in total silence,
Knowing that every move was intense.

The terror that hit downtown
Will be remembered all around.
Years on, looking back on that day,
We pay respect to those who died, we pray

'God be with their families as they mourn
For they cry as their family is torn.'

**Emma Montgomery (15)**
**Ballyclare High School**

# Go For The Gold

'On your marks!'
I crouch down on the uncomfortable little stones.
'Get set!'
I straighten my back leg, feeling uneasy, waiting for the last word.
'Go!'
I push off and move my arms and legs like crazy.

I keep my head up, forward, looking straight ahead,
Keeping my eyes in front of me,
Although, I can't help but realise I'm in the lead.
I pass the 100 metre mark,
I've still got 300 metres left to go,
I can't keep this up.

I slow down a little,
The wrong decision,
One, two, three people take over me,
I can't let the rest go ahead,
I push my body harder although I've a stitch in my side.

The burst of speed only lasts a second,
The last four people go ahead.
I'm *last*.

Past the 200 metre mark,
I run past two people finding a space in the inside lane,
I'm 6th.

I'm coming up to the 300 metre mark,
I can't let all my hard work go to waste,
I've been training for weeks.
I feel inspired and get a burst of energy,
I feel my body building up to full speed sprint.

I can see the finish line and everyone cheering.
There's just one other person in front.
20 metres away.
I'm in front,
No, she is,
I'm in front,
No, she is,
Yes, it's me in front,
I've won,
I've done it.
The gold medal is around my neck,
I've won the gold.

**Sarah Tilbury (13)**
**Ballyclare High School**


# Political Problems

What has our political system come to today?
Our leaders are liars and cause great dismay.
George Bush seldom knows what to say
And Tony Blair has thrown Britain into disarray.

I suppose his defence is that his hands are bound,
But his insidious twittering is such a frightful sound.
It might even bore some into voting against the pound!
Of course, Blair's so naive, he doesn't even know coins are round.

The first time it happened, the Gulf War was bad,
But going back there again, that was just mad!
When British soldiers died, was Bush even sad?
Was he happy he had become just like his dad?

So what's my opinion on the war in Iraq?
I think we should give Bush the sack!
To world peace and diplomacy, it was a stab in the back
And I am quite sure it's a job he just can't hack.

So, sorry Tony and George to burst your bubble,
But quite frankly, my dears, you're both in trouble.

**Emma Wilson (14)**
**Ballyclare High School**

# Time

It seems like only yesterday I was a little child,
All bundled up in my mother's arms.
I seemed to remember the way she gazed down
And kissed me on the head
Without fail, every night, before she went to bed.

Those days are gone, I'm older now,
I don't need a kiss goodnight.
I'm tired when I give out a yawn
So I head to bed without a fight.

My mother and I get on really well,
I can share everything with her,
About friends, school, even my problems,
I can always rely, she will always be there.

Schooldays are Monday to Friday,
Those days going really quick
With revising in-between,
Granny always said to knuckle down
There's no point living life with a frown,
Where does the time go?

When weekends come they're always a blast,
Oh how I wish they would only last.
It's a time to relax, reflect on the week,
Where does the time go?

Soon I will be even older,
Have a job, go to college, or perhaps even marriage.
I'll be an independent woman
In the wide world on my own,
Oh where does time go?

**Jenna Hamilton  (14)**
**Ballyclare High School**

# A Hockey Match

To battle we go while all still asleep,
Without a sound, all deep in thought,
Concentrating on the task at hand,
We try to remember all we've been taught . . .

A whistle blows, the signal is sounded,
Subtly we start the attack,
Precision passing performed without error,
Taking one step forward and two back.

As if drawn by a magnet we endlessly chase
A target of white on black,
The air is filled with shouts not moans
For determination we do not lack.

Tirelessly we run to support,
Greatly encouraged by our progress.
We decide to quicken the steady pace,
This decision meets instant success.

*Crack!* A gun to the hearts of the enemies,
Persistence was the key,
A reward for all our hard work
And a pat on the back for me.

We now advance with confident ease,
Strength, speed and skill.
We use each to our advantage as we see
The enemy give up the will.

All too soon a whistle blows
Like music to our ears.
We gather round our captain who
Triumphantly gives three cheers.

**Kim Montgomery (14)**
**Ballyclare High School**

# Unrequited Love

I hear you're winter calling out to me,
So cold and clear.
I feel your rain against my skin
And just as you resent her
I feel the pain of your sin.
Deep inside your heart is shamed
And I know nothing can ever be the same,
But we may seek the unseekable
And try to believe.

Her smile was sweet, her love sweeter still,
Yet her charms lay in the ways of sin.
You were blind, what could you do?
Warnings had no place in your love-struck eyes,
Your world was shattered by the sounds of love
And yet no help was sent from above.

But, still I am here to help you through,
Forget your mistakes, and lift yourself up
From that steep fall from grace.
Regret is a curse, there's nothing left to say,
So let's just run away and maybe someday
You will forget her,
And learn to love me again.

**Jennifer Dunn  (17)**
**Ballyclare High School**


# Winter

W inter winds blow the fluffy white snow
 I  cicles hang from Santa's sleigh as he goes, 'Ho! Ho!'
N ear the North Pole where snowmen are singing
T ime for Christmas bells to start ringing
E arly in the morning when children make a wish
R eindeer are eating out of a dish.

**Alison Crothers  (11)**
**Ballyclare High School**

# Friends

Friends are like our chosen family
Who we cherish no matter what.
They are special to us in every way
Because they help us through every day.

Friends help us whenever times are hard
And they are what matter most.
Friends forever we will always be
And I'll be there for you, no matter when you need me.

Together we support each other.
Remembering the things which bring us together,
Clothes, make-up, boys and hair.
We have so many things that we can share.

Friends we can always turn to
Even when we have moved on.
True friends will always be there
When everyone else has gone.

**Heather Bailie (17)**
**Ballyclare High School**


# Puppy Love

*To Grace from Sweep*

Lick, lick, wag, wag,
Wag, wag, lick, lick.
Woof, woof, whimper, whimper,
Whimper, whimper, woof, woof.

*To Sweep from Grace*

I love your little waggy tail,
Even your whimper and your wail.
I love your 'catch me' playful glance,
But best of all, your 'welcome home' dance.

**Grace Kennedy (12)**
**Ballyclare High School**

# Hallowe'en

That Hallowe'en I shan't forget
I'll even place a bet
That they're coming for me again.
Maybe they can hear me talking,
Even as my dog is barking.
The Angel of Death must not stay,
The Grim Reaper dare I say,
I told him to come back next May.

Satan and his minions aren't very nice,
Jesus come down and give them headlice,
They went to the chemist to get some shampoo.
A week later I got a postcard from Timbuktu.
The evil wizards and Voldemort,
The police came along and took 'em to court.
Then came the ghouls and ghosts,
I wasn't the best of hosts.
I called in the Ghostbusters and the NYPD and me.
And they all did flee
From the Ghostbusters and the NYPD.

The phantom came all depressed,
I told him he'd got the wrong address.
Pandora came with her box,
It turns out she's allergic to me,
She's got to get something for that allergy.
Then came Frankenstein, he rather stunk
So I gave him a bottle of Calvin Klein.
Dracula came and forgot his teeth and watch,
We had such a good time, till dawn.

Monsters beware, you're in for a scare
Because I have a pet grizzly bear.

**Ryan Cooke  (12)**
**Ballyclare High School**

# The Sea

The sea is as smooth as a rock
As I stand here watching from the dock.
I can see the fish swimming along,
This is the place where they belong.

The sea is as rough as gravel
As I watch the waves unravel.
I can hear the seals calling
As the heavy rain starts falling.

The sea roars like a lion
As I hear the dolphins crying.
The tide comes in and covers the sand,
The sea is now in command.

The sea is as blue as a sapphire,
This beautiful colour I admire.
I can smell the air is so fresh and clean,
This is the best place I've ever seen.

**Nicola Louise Rodgers  (13)**
**Ballyclare High School**


# Dolphins

D olphins diving here and there,
O ver the waves without a care

L azily gliding through the sea,
P erfect animals so gentle and free.

H appily they talk and play,
I n the water they frolic all day.

So elegant and graceful,
I think they're very peaceful.

N aturally beautiful and smart,
S urely a wonderful work of art.

**Dawn Comins  (12)**
**Ballyclare High School**

# What It's Like To Be A Ghost!

Have you ever wondered what it's like
Living in the afterlife?

Heaven or Hell the decision's been made,
The hopes of rebirth begin to fade.

Halfway between, neither good nor bad,
Purgatory is sure to be had.

If you find you're stuck in there,
There's only one way out, but beware.

Back to Earth as a ghost can be terribly daunting,
But unfinished business needs sorting.

Floating all day as free as a bird,
Never seen, never heard.

Existing like this can be terribly boring
Even when the rain is pouring.

Now comes the warning, I forgot to tell,
Being like this is a living Hell!

**Matthew Hunter  (12)**
**Ballyclare High School**


# Rugby

Rugby is a hard game.
You have to be rough and tough.
You have to be fast and furious.
You have to be fit and strong or you won't last long.

Who will win the Rugby World Cup, England or New Zealand?
I hope New Zealand will win, the fastest, fittest and most furious.

I also hope England will win because they are strong
And they've got Jonny Wilkinson, the perfect No 10.
The most expensive player in the World Cup is Jonny Wilkinson.

So who will win the World Cup?
We'll just have to wait and see.

**Scott Wylie  (12)**
**Ballyclare High School**

# The Wilderness Gave It To Me!

Within me there are many animals
But together they build up my personality.
I know this because the wilderness gave them to me!

There is a kitten in me. Full of fun and lots of joy
But shy and fragile to people unknown.
Little small paws and tiny feet
Always there with a small but happy greet.
I know this because the wilderness gave it to me!

There is a rabbit in me. All bouncy and happy
And looking for a great adventure.
Friendly and always there when you need someone to talk to.
It likes its food, nibble, nibble, nibble.
I know this because the wilderness gave it to me!

There is a puppy in me. Likes a laugh and lots of mischief
And is always there as a friend for life.
If you pass it in the street a bark and a wag of its tail
And that will be your greet.
I know this because the wilderness gave it to me!

There is a dolphin in me. Likes to play and splash about,
Swims all day and swims all night looking for its food.
It has smooth blue skin but it can be cold
And is normally as good as gold.
I know this because the wilderness gave it to me!

There is a lion in me. Very grumpy and very lazy too
And likes to lie in the sun before its work's all done.
Hunting for fun and hunting for food
Are its favourite things to do.
Bossy and will argue with anyone who doesn't listen.
I know this because the wilderness gave it to me!

There is a jungle of animals in me.
They might be big and some might be small
But they're very important to me because
*The wilderness gave them to me!*

**Emma Jayne Ferguson  (13)**
**Ballyclare High School**

# Friends

Friends are wonderful,
Friends are fun,
Friends are always No 1,
They make you laugh,
They make you smile
And never make you run a mile.

Friends are caring,
Friends are kind,
They're never off your mind.
Phoning you up every day and night
Telling you what they were up to last night.

Friends will never grass on you
Or tell you always what to do.
They share their problems and listen to yours,
They hate when they're made to do chores
Because then they can't go out.

**Rachel Smyth (12)**
**Ballyclare High School**


# Free

This is happiness,
Standing still with the wind
Playing with my hair
And the gentle breeze
Dancing over my face.
It's blowing away stress,
Tiredness, all my worries.
I feel carefree and light,
As if I'm flying.
On an empty beach I
Stand alone, letting go
Of everything I don't
Need in my life.
That's it, it's gone.
Once again I'm free . . .

**Joanne Williamson (12)**
**Ballyclare High School**

# An Old Man Dreaming

A little old man, alone in his haven,
Alone and quiet, thinking:
Thinking of his life, so many good times,
With his hands on his lap, he dreams.

Dreams of his adventures, wonderful thoughts,
His family, his friends and his foes,
His childhood events full of laughter and joy,
But this joy quickly moves on.

Nightmares now appear, awful and bad
With death in the sight of his eyes.
He thinks of the war, his allies in peril,
The death and the trauma, he survived.

With all those bad thoughts he thinks of death;
A light at the end of the tunnel.
How great it must be to live in Heaven,
With God so loving and giving.

**Ashleigh Holmes  (12)**
**Ballyclare High School**


# Hopefully Some Day

His eyes shone like a shimmer on the sea,
These jewels to be opened only by me,
He sees me in a way no other will know,
Hopefully some day he will be able to show.

People will look and people will talk,
But honestly, there is nothing there to mock,
For I am in love, and always will be,
Hopeful some day they all will see.

Maybe he'll be mine, or maybe he'll not,
But I will always dream and give it a thought,
Deep down inside I know he feels the same,
Hopeful some day his love and mine will reign.

**Joanna Caldwell  (17)**
**Ballyclare High School**

# Why Oh Why?

When I go down to the sea
And see the golden sand
The thought always comes to mind
What's happened to this land?

The world was once one big family
Joined together to unite
But when it started to split up the timing was just right
War began to take its place
Over things like money, land and race.

When I go down to the sea
And see the golden sand
The thought always comes to mind
What's happened to this land?

Centuries over centuries started moving fast
But now we're in the modern world
It's the 21st century at last
When I see people fighting
It disgraces me inside
Why can't there just be peace
Can these people not abide?

When I go down to the sea
And see the golden sand
The thought always comes to mind
What's happened to this land?

**Suzanne Weir  (13)**
**Ballyclare High School**

# Twilight

There is magic in the twilight
And it fills me with delight,
A yawning half-dimension,
Is this time of dark and light.

Skin cracks and tingles in the gloom
And there are those that say
That the Devil walks on water
When it's neither night nor day.

The secrets of the mother
Under this lacy veil,
Are revealed to me in whispers
Among the shadows pale,
And I cannot fight the feeling
That there's something I just miss
As I rove my eyes to witness
As the Earth receives night's kiss.

So say a prayer for those who miss it
And those who see it not,
The beauty of the quiet child
That the day and night begot.

**Caroline Montgomery  (17)**
**Ballyclare High School**


# Summer

The sun shining so bright
Like a diamond in the light
A sunflower sitting in a pot
Placed in a certain spot
The ducks and swans
Swimming in the ponds
Seeing the green, green grass
Whilst driving past
I wish summer stayed forever
Because I don't like winter.

**James Bones  (11)**
**Ballyclare High School**

# Shopping With My Mum

Whenever I go out
shopping with my mum,
we're always in M&S
or Marks and Sparks - that's the one.

I hate inside Primark
it's always a bore.
It's just like the rest,
BHS and Dunnes Stores.

Then there's Boots
and Mothercare too.
When my mum shops
there's too much to do.

I like some shops
like Virgin Megastore.
But that Next in Belfast,
it's got too many floors.

Then we will stop somewhere
for a bite to eat,
but we're late thanks to Next
and we can't find a seat.

Once we have come out
from eating our food
my mum's shopping is over,
now it's my turn - good.

My mum will then ask,
'Where do you want to go?'
'Oh, HMV, Virgin, Game,
I don't know.'

'Right then, I'll take you to one.'
'Fine, OK, then I'll go to Game.'
When we get there, too late, it's shut -
no doubt about it, clothes shops are to blame.

**Ryan Glass (13)**
**Ballyclare High School**

# The Win

With 2 minutes left of the final
Peterson receives the ball down the right wing,
Runs 3/4 of the pitch,
Carries it in a little,
Plays a one-two with Adams,
About to pass to Reynolds
Who was about to score the winning goal.
The crowd's on the edge of their seats
Biting their nails,
Anderson comes in with a dirty tackle,
Ref points straight to the spot
And shows the red card.
The crowd boos Anderson off the pitch
And chants to him: 'Cheerio, cheerio, cheerio.'
Dobbs steps up to take,
The tension is so bad you could cut it with a knife,
You could see his heart pumping,
All of a sudden he took it,
We sat anxiously, straight into the top corner.
Everyone jumping for joy. The whole stand got up
And onto the pitch for the biggest pitch invasion ever.
We had won the league, the league,
It was unreal.

**Adam Sharratt  (14)**
**Ballyclare High School**


# Flowers

F  antastic coloured flowers
    make any plant look dazzling.
L  ovely scents make the flower smell amazing.
O  dour of great sensation.
W  hether the weather is wonderful or not
    they can always cheer you.
E  ach petal formed to perfection.
R  each out to our sensations.

**Emma Gault  (11)**
**Ballyclare High School**

# Man United

We are Man United
The best team in the land,
We're way ahead of all the rest
So catch us if you can.

'Keano, Keano!'
The Stretford end cries.
Wee Paul Scholes has got a goal!
As the other team's fans sigh.

The red-faced Alex Ferguson
Barking orders from the bench,
'Keep a good attacking line
And keep focused in defence.'

We've all got star quality
From Ruud up front to Rio at the back
And the midfield is always there
To pick up any slack.

Other fools might disagree
But I don't give a hoot
Because we are the champions
And Ruud's got the golden boot.

So easily we are the best
It's plain for all to see,
With Ronaldo's tricks and Giggsy's pace
We'll finish top of the league.

**Chris McNeill  (14)**
**Ballyclare High School**

# Monday Blues

Our house is always in such a fuss
'Cause everyone's in such a rush.
We wash our faces
And grab our cases,
So as not to miss the bus.

When in school we feel uncool;
French, German, biology,
Maths, English, technology,
We'd rather be in a pool.

When the bell rings
Our hearts all go ding.
As we rush out of class
We get such a blast,
We just want to joyfully sing.

When at home when we are fed,
We snuggle into our cosy beds.
We say our prayers,
Of all our cares
And worry not of Monday's dread.

**Catherine Vennard  (14)**
**Ballyclare High School**


# Incredible Eagle

I'd love to be an eagle,
To fly high up in the air
And swoop down low to catch some fish
With amazing grace and flair.

I'd love to use my great sharp talons,
My mighty, dark brown wings
And fly so high up to the clouds,
Above where all the birds sing.

**Matthew Lok  (11)**
**Ballyclare High School**

# Water

A precious resource, taken for granted
Ebbs and flows over the Earth

Swirling, surging, splashing

Used for cooking, cleaning,
Washing and rinsing

Rippling, rushing, running

Its power unleashed in tidal waves
Bringing destruction and then tranquillity

Swirling, surging, splashing

Devouring our coastlines
Consuming clifftop homes

Gushing, gulping, gobbling

A vital commodity
Refreshing the world, plants and people

Rippling, rushing, running

Clear, clean, transparent
Reflecting light like crystal

Swirling, surging, splashing

Until pollution spoils its beauty
Toxic and tainted

Soiled, spoiled, stained

Where it once gave life it will now take
Lifeless fish lie on an oozing tide.

**John Millar  (16)**
**Ballyclare High School**

# Night-Time

I lie in the darkness
All alone,
Wondering, thinking,
What will happen next?

I toss and turn
In my bed,
Trying to sleep
Before it becomes day.

Thoughts run wildly
Through my head,
I can't stop thinking
But I want to sleep.

I feel so tired,
Yet am still awake,
I start to worry,
Will I never sleep?

The night grows older
But I'm not asleep,
It is so dark
And is so scary.

I hear voices
But shut them out,
Soon I am in the place
I want to be in.

**Claire Gaffney  (14)**
**Ballyclare High School**

# September

School is coming once again,
No more getting up at lunchtime,
No more leisurely strolls in the sun,
No more freedom of wearing what you want,
No more evenings in front of the telly.

Instead it's back to the old routine,
Alarms set for early mornings,
Wet and windy walks to school,
Homework to be done for next day,
Deadlines set for the not-so-distant future,
Never-ending science lessons and detentions looming,
Late nights writing English essays,
Staring blankly at computer screens,
Maths exercises and French learning.

But then it's all over,
The weekend has come,
A time to relax,
Until Monday morning at least.

**Edmund Davis (15)**
**Ballyclare High School**


# The Baby

I know a little baby,
Laura is her name.
Things were quiet and peaceful
Till to our house she came.

Although she's very tiny
She makes her presence felt.
She yells and cries and wriggles
But she would make your heart melt.

Of course we really love her,
She's gorgeous through and through
And if you called to see her
I know you would love her too.

**David Mairs (11)**
**Ballyclare High School**

*Young Writers - Poetry In Motion Co Antrim*

# School: My View

We come in our droves
By no choice of our own
And sit all day bored,
Dreaming of home.

Uniforms like prison suits,
Food that's half the price,
Teachers are like warders,
Classrooms are our quarters.

Every day the same old things
But science and maths are my favourite things.
All the rest I have no use for,
Frankly, they are quite a bore.

No talking, no running,
Might as well not smile.
The only thing that keeps me going
Is the presence of friends.

Don't start me on the head,
How much does he get paid
To sit all day and watch
As we do all the work?

Some of the teachers are brilliant,
Others shouldn't be let near kids.
Sometimes I really pity them
For putting up with us!

But in the end I have no say
And have to come in too,
Until the end of this year that is,
Then it's up to me,
Hee, hee.

**William Andrews (16)**
**Ballyclare High School**

# The Sun

It will always come,
It will always go,
You can rely on it
To always show.

Without it
You could never see,
If it didn't exist
Life couldn't be.

It makes you feel happy
'Cause it's bold and bright.
When it's not out
Some feel a fright.

It rises in the east
And sets in the west,
I think you've now
Started to guess.

If it never came
Life would be no fun,
Yes, you've got it,
It's the sun.

**Jayne Cluff  (14)**
**Ballyclare High School**


# Winter

Santa comes at this time of year
and he brings his team of reindeer.

The land is white and covered with snow
and Santa always says, 'Ho! Ho! Ho!'

The days are dark, the moon is bright
and it's always freezing cold at night.

The day's cold, the trees are bare;
no one knows the snowman's there!

**Adrian Hughes  (12)**
**Ballyclare High School**

# The Witch

One cold night, a witch came out
Looking for something tasty,
*How about a nice little boy or a lovely crispy pastie?*
Thought the witch to herself.

With this in mind, she crept up to a house
In her clothes all ragged, grey and torn.
Just then she saw a boy who looked quite forlorn,
Her vicious mind thought, *I'll pretend to mourn!*

The witch then said, 'Come to my lair
And I'll give you a nice, juicy, green pear.'
So the boy agreed to come
But when the witch said, 'I'm going to eat you!'
The boy screamed, 'I want my mum!'

**Zoë Scott (11)**
**Ballyclare High School**


# Food

My favourite food is Irish stew,
It is made with vegetables and beef
And is good for you.
The animals that beef come from go moo!
You should try it too!
It is full of vitamins that are essential to you.

My least favourite food is Brussels spouts,
They make my throat shout,
I need to get them out!
Please don't give them to me or I will shout,
They are green like cabbage and remind you of bouncy balls,
So you could chuck them at the wall!

**Alex Hagan (11)**
**Ballyclare High School**

# I Have A Monster Crush On You

I have a monster crush on you,
A super dinosaur,
It sits upon my chest and head
And yet I beg for more.

Whenever you're gone I miss you so,
My heart is so, so bland,
Yet when you're here, my stupid fear
Won't let me touch your hand.

I cannot eat, I cannot sleep,
I'm so amazed by you.
My thoughts fly up into the sky
And fade out of the blue.

I know this crush is not your fault
This mega dinosaur is mine,
But if you please could rescue me
And hold me and love me.

**Graeme Farquhar  (11)**
**Ballyclare High School**


# What If?

What if the world was flat?
What if the sky was green?
What if the grass was orange?
What if the sun was blue?

What if I was born first
Or never born at all?
What if I were taller
Or really, really small?

Would my life be the same
If the world was upside down
Or even inside out?
I don't think it would
But it'd be fun all the same.

**Ruth Young  (12)**
**Ballyclare High School**

# The Kitten

I have a little kitten,
He's coloured grey and white,
His whiskers have not grown yet,
They're still just out of sight.

He gets up to all the mischief
When he plays around the house,
But yet when he becomes a cat
We hope he'll kill a mouse.

He laps up all the milk we have,
His stomach never full,
And he plays with mother's knitting
And tangles up all her wool.

He chases all the chickens
Round and round the yard,
You'd think it was the panther
From the Ballybogey ward.

**Stuart Crawford (12)**
**Ballyclare High School**


# Summer

S ummer is my favourite time of year,
   the flowers are in full bloom.
U mbrellas are not needed,
   for summertime is here.
M others with their children
   are playing in the park.
M y pony and I go galloping
   over the lush green fields till dark.
E veryone is happy, the sky is clear and blue,
   the sun is shining bright for me and you.
R emember in the winter, when nights
   are long and dreary,
   summertime will soon be here,
   to stop us feeling weary.

**Rosie Ramsey (11)**
**Ballyclare High School**

# Seasons

In the spring lambs are born
And farmers start to sow corn,
Leaves on trees start to reappear
And summer is growing ever near.

In the summer I like to play
In the garden where the flowers are gay,
With my sisters we enjoy the sun,
So come on people and enjoy the fun.

In the autumn time leaves start to fall
And lots of flowers become really small,
They shrivel up and turn crispy and brown
And their heads droop sadly towards the ground.

In the wintertime the trees are bare
And the ground has an extra layer,
So don't go out, you might freeze,
Catch a cold and start to sneeze.

**Emma McAllister (12)**
**Ballyclare High School**


# Colours To Me

Blue to me are things bright and new,
Yellow to me is from me to you,
Purple means all the things in the ground,
Pink means everything is just sound.

Black means everything is so grey
And red means dream all of today,
Navy is when the night is found,
But green means everything is bound.

White is when everything is plain
And silver means I might be in pain,
Orange is when everything is OK,
But gold means dream all of today!

**Rebecca Archbold (11)**
**Ballyclare High School**

# Mums

Mums are loving, caring and helpful,
Mums can be angry, nagging and strict,
But mums are always there.
Mums can be short, mums can be tall,
Some are fat, some are slim,
But mums are always there.
Mums are there to pick you up from school,
Mums are there to wash, iron, cook and clean,
Mums don't care because they're always there.
If you've spilt your drink
Or dropped your toast and made a mess
Mums are always there.
If your sister's crying or your dad's late for tea
Mums just get on with things,
They don't care cos they're always there.
In the morning, noon and night
Mums are always there.

**Trevor McClintock (12)**
**Ballyclare High School**


# Six Pirates

Six pirates are on a pirate ship
Sailing the wide but deep sea.
Soon their ship sinks thanks to a crack
And that is the end of the pirate ship.

The pirates decide to take revenge
But in order to avenge their ship
They might need a cannon or two,
So they go to the shop, but don't find anything new.

So instead they get pistols, bullets a few
And walk up to the repaired ship
And shoot rounds at the crack, for all they're worth
And the pirate ship sinks all over again.

**Daryl Dundee (11)**
**Ballyclare High School**

# My House

This is a poem about a house of mine,
Up Seskin Avenue, number nine,
As you come and approach my gates
You will see the houses of my mates.

In the garden getting a tan
Is a wooden fisherman,
There he stands, tall and manly
And my mum calls him Stanley.

Walk up the steps and open the door,
Just let me tell you one thing more,
My little dog Tobyjack
Can hear even the slightest crack.

Here he comes running at you
And you'll be thinking what to do,
Just pat and stroke his head
And he will go back to bed.

Into the living room sitting there
Are three small ornamental bears,
Each one has a certain birthstone,
My dad's, my mum's and even my own.

Go into the dining room and into the hall,
It isn't too big, it is quite small,
If you turn to the left and not the right,
Should I show you my favourite room? I think I might.

As you can probably guess
This room can sometimes be a mess,
It is my room, a room of blue
And in it sits my PlayStation 2.

The carpet is blue,
The wallpaper too,
My GameCube sits with all its games,
All of them have different names.

**Christopher Craig (11)**
**Ballyclare High School**

# Autumn

I sit on the branch of my tallest tree
And say to myself, 'It cannot be.'
One leaf, two leaves, three leaves, four
All fall to the foot of my front door.

I go for a walk to clear my head,
Then I see a hedgehog in its bed.
Then a rabbit in its little burrow
With its family sleeping in a row.

A car is coming, so I have to wait
Then it hits me, it's the time I hate.

Yes, summer's gone and winter's here,
No more fishing on the pier.
Hallowe'en is still to come,
So we'll all have lots of fun.

**Ross D Vint**
**Ballyclare High School**

# The Butterfly

What an attractive butterfly,
She's basking in the sun,
She soars up high into the sky,
It appears to be quite fun.

I yearn to hover above
All the vegetation,
I would love to spread my wings,
I could use my imagination.

But really if the truth be told
Perhaps it's just my dream,
A butterfly as large as me
Would cause my mum to scream.

**Rachel Brown (11)**
**Ballyclare High School**

# Someone Cares

Alone she stands alone and waiting,
For a call she will not hear.
This girl in London is only deaf and dumb.
She stands there waiting with the other slum.

Her silent tears run down her cheeks,
No one in this world does care
About this little, small girl,
Deaf, dumb and fair.
Left in the streets all day long,
No home, no love, no care.
But if she could ever talk,
She'd say life is unfair.

Still to this day the girl is waiting,
For a call she will not hear.
But this girl inside is strong
And will always long
To hear and talk to someone who cares.

But now someone does care
And messages sent through the air,
Reach down to this little girl.
Spirits she never knew
Warm her up inside!
How cannot she see
That they are there,
Helping her survive?

Although she may not know it,
Someone, somewhere
Will always care!

**Catriona Luney (11)**
**Ballyclare High School**

# A Dream Of Elephants

I dreamed a dream of elephants,
I cannot tell you why,
But in my dream I saw the herd
Go slowly walking by.

They moved beneath a blazing sun,
Through rising dust and heat.
They made their solemn journey
On strong and silent feet.

As I watched the steady herd
Walked slowly, sadly by,
Until I stood, amazed, alone
Beneath a silent sky.

I watched them as they moved away,
I watched as they walked on.
They merged into the heat and dust
Till all of them were gone.

I dreamed a dream of elephants,
I cannot tell you why,
But in my dreams I saw the herd
Go slowly walking by.

**Rachael Bailie (11)**
**Ballyclare High School**

# The Senses

What can I hear? What can I hear?
I can hear a rap at the door,
And a mouse under the floor.
Oh what wonderful things to hear.

What can I see? What can I see?
I can see a rabbit in a hole
And a man carrying coal.
Oh what wonderful things to see.

What can I touch? What can I touch?
I can touch my sister's doll
And also the switch in the hall.
Oh what wonderful things to touch.

What can I smell? What can I smell?
I can smell my lovely pork chop
And my jelly beans from the shop.
Oh what wonderful things to smell.

What can I speak? What can I speak?
I can speak the word of God
And tell my mum I won't eat cod.
Oh what wonderful things to speak.

**Kyle Clarke (12)**
**Ballyclare High School**

# Snakes

Long and venomous a snake can be,
In the tall grass they are hard to see.
Squiggly and powerful it moves around,
Dominating the area around.

Hard and tough the crushing python is,
Giving off a large hiss.
Stunning and striking a snake can be,
In a life of stealth, oh hard it must be.

**Lee Coupe (13)**
**Ballyclare High School**

# Stargazing

I look into the sky at night
And wonder at the distant light
Piercing through the empty void
Of all air and gravity, devoid.

Travelling faster than the speed of sound
Faster than anything on the ground
From a solar system far, far away
Until it reached our planet, this very day.

Countless billions of miles away
There is another planet, starting another day.
Maybe similar to ours
Maybe seeing a billion other stars.

The distances are never-ending
Far beyond my comprehending.
If every star is another sun
Surely there's another planet like our own?

**Andrew Mahon (15)**
**Ballyclare High School**


# Christmas Eve

It was Christmas Eve, we were very excited
We were waiting for the man in the big, red suit
It was Christmas Eve and we were enlightened
We were waiting for the man with all the loot
We are little boys and we're waiting for the man with all the toys
We can't wait to eat that pud
For at Christmas, we are little hoods
We like to rummage through all the presents
And tell our friends who live down the Crescent
It is Christmas Eve and we are very excited
For we little boys, are enlightened.

**Jordan Watson (11)**
**Ballyclare High School**

# Grandad

He is a proud man of more than three score years and ten
and hopes he'll last to make a century.
He's good at telling yarns and often shares stories
of his youth with me.

He stands a good six foot three and in his heyday
was a big, strong man on the footplate of the
'Number 81 - Carrickfergus Castle' express passenger train,
which often made its way from Belfast to Larne Harbour.

His silver hair is always neatly groomed but is going rather thin on top
he always has a healthy glow and a smile to greet you.
A cross word seldom leaves his lips.

He tackles tasks, both large and small
and works with great enthusiasm and determination.
His nimble, green fingers have nurtured many plants and shrubs
in his ornamental garden.

His endless energy puts us all to shame,
he dreams up jobs and plans them in advance.
Is never bored on rainy days. He's an expert now,
in household chores.

Like an elephant, he never forgets . . . well on a rare occasion!
I'm proud of him, just as he is so proud of me!

He's the best friend I'll ever have - that's Grandad!

**Jonathan Steenson  (14)**
**Ballyclare High School**

# Letting Go

Time passes quickly
And I'll grow with change,
But it's only the beginning
So I'm finding it strange.

I'm a sensitive person
My heart's on my sleeve
People around wonder
Why I ponder and grieve.

But I've stacks of memories
That'll never disappear
For they're embedded in me
And shine through so clear.

I remember all the things
That made me laugh or cry,
And I remember everything you said
Up until our final goodbye.

So when people pass in my life
So quickly, to and fro
I have to finally learn
That it's time to let go.

**Jane McAllister (15)**
**Ballyclare High School**

# My Poem

In a girl's head there would be a fly, but
it would be dead
Because of all the make-up they put on
their head!

Girls have this thing with talking. They talk while
working, while playing and while walking.

They do nothing but talk, talk, talk, talk,
talk and don't forget talk!

But some who are shy don't go on and on
about clothes or boys or make-up.
They read, work, read, work and also read while working.

They are so boring but as for boys, they are sporty,
clever, hardworking (some) and most of all
the superior race.

**Michael Carson  (14)**
**Ballyclare High School**


# Santa

I write my list to Santa,
When Christmas time comes near,
He brings me lots of presents,
In the sleigh pulled by his reindeer.

When Santa comes to my house,
He brings me lots of toys,
Barbies for the girls
And footballs for the boys.

When Santa comes to my house,
The reindeer pulls the sleigh.
I always leave cookies, carrots and milk,
To help them on their way.

**Kyle Patterson  (13)**
**Ballyclare High School**

# My Zoo

I live in Parkgate
And this is where
My zoo began
But with no monkeys or bears
I got a dog when I was two
This was the beginning of my zoo.
I won a fish at a fair
I still stop to wonder and stare.
Then my two cats
Who pounce, scratch, dig up and bury
My naughty little friends are called Shaggy and Purry.
The hamster was next, it gave me fits
It was always me that it scratched to bits.
So that was the end of that little rodent
The pet shop is where it went.
A snake slithered in
But sadly it died long and thin.
It belonged to my brother
It was very sad, so we got another.
Then a rabbit came my way
That was a very happy day.
It was as friendly as could be
It only brought me happiness and glee.
Then we got a pony
What fun to jump and gallop.
When I heard it was coming
My heart gave a hop
I wanted a chinchilla for me and you
But my mum called out,
'No more additions to our zoo!'

**Suzanne Whan (12)**
**Ballyclare High School**

# Is She Gone?

Granny used to come round
Now she doesn't.
At first she was well
But then she wasn't.

She got a lot better
But then she got worse.
Mummy was crying
It was like a curse.

Mummy cried more and more
And Daddy got mad.
Granny didn't come back
And then Dad was sad.

We went to a big building
And there we saw Gran.
She was quiet and still
She couldn't stand.

Her tummy went up
And it went down.
Her eyes closed once more
And her hand hit the ground.

I saw her again
Everyone was in black.
Mummy was crying again
Was Gran coming back?

Gran stopped coming
I asked Mum where she was.
Mum said she was in Japan
Teacher said she's in Oz.

Once I was awoken
It was just past dawn.
I cried about Gran
Is she gone?

**Nicola Abernethy (12)**
**Ballyclare High School**

# The Match

We climb the great big steps
And burst onto the scene.
A field of blue is spread across,
No empty seat is seen.

Saturday at Stamford Bridge,
It's the great big match.
Mutu comes onto the pitch,
He's the one to watch.

The players come on to applause
And split to take their marks.
Shouting starts, tension mounts,
The whistle's blown to start.

A player scores a goal
For everyone to see.
We're 1-0 up, the players crowd,
Like a swarm of bees.

We're feeling good,
Mutu does a run.
He dodges and he scores,
To us another one.

It's near the end,
We clap and chant.
The whistle goes, we won 2-0,
That's what we want.

**Julie McCormick (15)**
**Ballyclare High School**

# Sports I Play

Some days I play rugby,
The rough and aggressive sport.
I play on the outside of the scrum
And wait for the ball to go out wide.

We then break up
And run up the field
We've got the ball, so we score a try
And now we lead the game.

On other days I play football
The more easy-going game.
I like to win the tackles
And get the ball cleared.

When we have possession
We get the ball out wide.
A cross comes in, we score a goal,
Now it's 1-0, hip, hip, hooray.

After the matches,
There's cheers all around.
Whether we've won or lost
But we know we did our best!

**Glenn McMaster  (12)**
**Ballyclare High School**

# The Lonely Hamster

The lonely hamster was calm,
He lived in the desert.
He went out one balmy night,
He took a turn, not merely right.

He found food to his delight,
He went back and lost his way.
A bird swooped low that night,
As the sun rose he was hit by a ray.

He waited until dead of night,
He went then to continue his roam.
He went back and took the turn right,
He found himself at his own true home.

**Craig Reed (12)**
**Ballyclare High School**


# A Strange Story

A saw a pigeon making bread!
I saw a girl composed of thread!
I saw a towel one mile square!
I saw a meadow in the air!
I saw a pony make a file!
I saw a blacksmith in a box!
I saw an orange kill an ox!
I saw a butcher made of steel!
I saw a penknife dance a reel!
I saw a sailor 12 feet high!
I saw a ladder in a pie!
I saw an apple fly away!
I saw a sparrow making hay!
I saw 3 men who saw these too
And will confirm what I tell you!

**Danielle McIlwaine (11)**
**Belfast Royal Academy**

# You Were My Light

I'm flyin' high when your near me,
I touch the sky when we're together,
you know you light my way
when I'm alone
I hope my light don't ever go out in the dark.

Just like I wish our love won't lose the sparks,
from the 1st time we met walkin' down the street,
you looked at me and passion pumped through my heart,
started beatin like never b4,
those deep, brown eyes of yours,
they seem so soft and sweet,
but yet they pierced my soul and sent me spinning
with a feelin like I was in Heaven.

I'm flyin' high when you're near me,
I touch the sky when we're together,
you know you light my way
when I'm alone
I hope my light don't ever go out in the dark.

Then suddenly my light went out one night when we went to bed,
I woke up and you had gone,
my life was in darkness
and I felt scared, alone and empty,
but soon I realised I could light my own way through my life,
I just hope now you're not beside me, I'll be strong on my own.

I was flyin' high when you were near me,
I touched the sky when we were together,
you lit my way when I was alone,
I hoped my light never went out in the dark.

But when it did I lit my own light,
for the dark,
without you.

**Danielle Magee  (14)**
**Belfast Royal Academy**

# The Battles Of Sierra Leone

The day of reckoning was upon him,
The day we hoped
Would never come
Today he would kill.

Soon hundreds of people's
Screams would chill the air,
As the rebel army
Approached the village.

Now the rebel gunfire
Pierced air, land and flesh.
With villagers running and screaming,
The shots continued.

It was not long ago
That he was one of those villagers,
Fleeing for his life.
As the rebels attacked his village.

His parents perished then,
Yet they were the fortunate ones,
They were not forced to fight.
He could not do this.

As a rebel explosion,
Shuddered the land,
He drove his bayonet,
Through his chest.

And for him,
The battles of Sierra Leone
Ceased.

**Steven Laverty  (13)**
**Belfast Royal Academy**

# Midnight Sky

M idnight has come
I can see it and feel it
D arkness has arisen
N ow that I am in the country, there is no light
I feel the wind gushing past my face
G reat light comes from the moon and the stars
H elping me to see the beautiful midnight sky
T onight Mars is the closest it has ever been

S kylines become red, Mars is coming
K eep dreaming that you will see it again
Y et you can see it everywhere, here is the best.

**Nicole Edwards (11)**
**Belfast Royal Academy**


# A Reflection In A Window

When you look out the window, what do you see?
I see trees and birds, the sky and the soil,
What does this mean?
Nothing I see, what do you see
You see cars and buildings, walls and fences,
Do you understand?
When you daydream
It's of only money and the things you want to get
I think of people and how they live their lives
Wow! You understand and now you see my point
You don't see out the window, you only see what I don't.

**Daniel Rice (14)**
**Belfast Royal Academy**

# The Twin Towers

It started just a normal day,
People commuting to work and play,
No one suspected, no one guessed,
That today the world would be put to the test.
9/11 was the date,
That most of us now have come to hate.
The Twin Towers stood like a constellation in the sky
And yet they were targets of terrorism and malign.

At 8.45am, New York local time,
The first plane hit and no one thought it was a crime.
'A horrendous accident,' many said,
But a few hours later, thousands would be dead.

The second plane hit, people began to suspect,
That someone out there had a lack of respect.
They waited and prayed for the news to come
And when it did, they suddenly felt numb.

And so two years on, the world shall remember,
What a terrible day that was in September.
Although the culprit has not yet been caught,
We must remember what we have been taught.

**Edward Duffy  (14)**
**Belfast Royal Academy**


# The Steam Train

Like a huge iron monster
Rumbling across the horizon
On tracks of silver and planks of bronze
The flames so golden burn within it
Snow-white clouds puff out of it
The high-pitched whistle echoes around it
That is the steam train.

**David Costley  (11)**
**Belfast Royal Academy**

# My Home

Here at my home Tannybrake
There's lots to do each day,
Helping Dad on the farm
As well as games to play.

Feeding and milking the cows
Now I like doing that,
But Skippy and Speckles the calves
Keep licking my fingers and hat.

Suzy the small pony
Is much too fat,
More exercise, less grass
She'll not like that.

Patch the old dog
Carries my shoes to his bed,
When Sam the young collie
Prefers to chew sticks instead.

Sooty my big, black cat
He catches birds and mice,
But Lucy the tortoiseshell lady
Lies on the sofa so pretty and nice.

Life on the farm
Is busy all year through,
For animals, pets and people
Have all so much to do!

**Ruth Barr (14)**
**Cambridge House Grammar School**

# The Book

Daunting, distressing, dire
The room had a feeling of dread.
The child was drawn to the desk
Against her will, but inside her head
Her only thought was, *I can't, I won't.*

Daunting, distressing, dire
For you see on that desk lay
The book that had all the answers
Which would be needed some day
By the one who was scared to look.

Daunting, distressing, dire
The child reached the doorway
Crossed the threshold and went to the desk
'This is it, this is the day,'
She said as she reached the book.

Daunting, distressing, dire
She ran her hand over the old book
Obviously this was the way it was meant to be
She turned the pages to take a look
To see that her fate was . . .

**Claire McAuley (16)**
**Cross And Passion College**


# Pop! Bang!

There was an old out of cake
He stuffed it in the oven
And put it to bake.

The oven was too hot
He baked it too much
His eyes went *pop!*
His head went *bang!*
And that was the end of that old man.

**Emma Dickson (12)**
**Crumlin High School**

# Hallowe'en

Hallowe'en is here
Filling everyone with cheer
Full moon and black cats
Warty noses and pointy hats.

Pumpkins glow in the dark
Children playing and having a lark
Time to have a trick or treat
Will their bags be full of sweets?

The monsters are here to come and scare
Screams of terror fill the air!
Gremlins and vampires want a bite or two
Hope you don't end up in the witches' stew!

Don't worry, it's only for fun
The moon will go down and we'll see the sun
All the children will be safe and sound
Knowing there's really *no* monsters around.

**Michael Rees (12)**
**Crumlin High School**


# The Autumn Breeze

The autumn breeze feels like it is going to freeze
Because the leaves scatter on the ground
When you hear the sound of the breeze in the trees
This breeze gets sooooo cold, it feels like it is going to freeze.
When the leaves scatter, your teeth will chatter
And you are scared because you have heard the autumn breeze
But when you turn around and see
If you have found the autumn breeze,
There is nothing but the leaves on the ground.

**Sarah Campbell (12)**
**Crumlin High School**

# Happy Birds

I'm sitting in the classroom,
Outside it's dark and grey.
I look out the window
And see the little birds at play.

The rain is falling heavy,
But the birds don't seem to care.
They are splashing in the water
And flying in the air.

They are cleaning at their feathers,
Giving themselves a shiny coat.
Here comes a big crow swimming along,
He looks like he is going to burst into a song.

A few crows, sparrows and a dove or two,
A couple of robin redbreasts perched on an old shoe,
And watch the doves as they splash and coo.
They look a real motley crew.

The sun is now coming out,
They spread their wings to dry.
The birds give themselves a shake
And off they will all fly.

**Brendan Scollay (11)**
**Crumlin High School**


# The Two Birds

I saw two birds playing on a roof,
*Splash, splash, splash,* as they play together.
They were taking a rest while watching their nest,
It is quite hot and they are enjoying the weather.

The cat is looking up on the roof
Licking her lips
And thinking, *oh food!*

**Robert McCallister (11)**
**Crumlin High School**

# My Name

A listair means protector of mankind.
L ots of people call me Ali for short.
I love football and farming.
S wimming, I enjoy.
T ractors are terrific.
A chieve a high standard at school.
I am eleven years old.
R ed is my favourite colour.

M y favourite drink is cola.
C ars are class, especially those that go fast.
K etchup, I take on almost everything.
N orman is my middle name.
I n school, PE is my favourite subject.
G reat I am at art, so I'm told.
H ave two brothers older than me.
T wenty-five is my favourite number.

**Alistair McKnight (11)**
**Crumlin High School**


# About Me

L aura Ross is my name,
A nd writing poems is my game
U sually I'm quite bright and cheery
R arely am I dull and dreary
A nimals are my favourite things.

R abbits, dogs and birds that sing
O ranges, apples, bananas too
S weets and crisps I like to chew
S pecial girl, that is me.

**Laura Ross (11)**
**Crumlin High School**

# All About Me

When I look up at the stars,
I wonder about my mind's powers.
What can I do or what am I capable of?

It makes me wonder who I am.
And gets my thoughts flowing, like a river dam,
Trying to break through.
And I begin to ponder who is this girl?

Then I say I'm a girl in high school,
Who might not be very cool?
But can't wait, until she has completed her goals.

Wait a minute! I'm starting to think I'm . . .
A mbitious
N oisy, ha, ha!
D emanding
R eady for most
E nergetic
A musing.

I'm me!

**Andrea Hurley  (12)**
Crumlin High School


# The Birds

Sitting in class
Will time pass?
Suddenly a splash
Mrs McGary laughs
The birds were having a bath
In a puddle on the school roof!
Splashing and thrashing
Squawking and flying
*The birds were having a bath!*

**Emily Wakeling  (11)**
Crumlin High School

# Birds

The summer breeze
Caresses the trees,
As the birds splash and bathe in the morning sun
They look like they're having lots of fun
I wish I could join them.

They swim and play,
Even though the sky is grey
And the sun is starting to fade
I wish I could join them.

Now the leaves have fallen
The wind halts to a still,
The snow begins to fall
The winter starts to chill.

The chirping has all ended
The swimming has all stopped.
The sun has disappeared
So they fly somewhere hot.
I wish I could join them . . .

**Georgie Brown (12)**
**Crumlin High School**


# My Poem

S tephanie is my name,
T alking is my game.
E ncouraged by my mother,
P urple is my favourite colour.
H airdressing I'd like to do
A nd have my own salon too.
N orthern Ireland is where I was born,
I n the summer I went to Lorne.
E very day I breathe!

**Stephanie Patterson (12)**
**Crumlin High School**

# Michelle

M is for me
I will always be
C is for care
H appy and bare
E is for eligible
L ovely and legible
L is for loads
E lephants and toads

P is for Price
R hymes with rice
I is for ice
C old and nice
E is for everyone I know.

**Michelle Price (11)**
**Crumlin High School**


# Little Birds

A little bird is flying
from that tree,
Is he flying over me?

I love its feathers
And its little, yellow beak,
Can he play hide and go seek?

He is swimming like a duck,
he looks so beautiful,
Did he get rid of all the muck?

Look at that little bird
hopping around,
I love its chirping sound.

**April Ingram (11)**
**Crumlin High School**

# A Poem About Me

T is for my name Thomas.
H is for my many hobbies.
O is for the way that I observe.
M is for me.
A is for my abilities.
S is for my favourite hobby, sports.

M is for my best possession, my mobile.
C is for my favourite drink, Coke.
D is for my brother's name, Daniel.
O is for my favourite monkey, an orang-utan.
N is for my favourite sports top maker, Nike.
N is for my nice attitude.
E is for what I get in school, education.
L is for the football team I dislike, Liverpool.
L is for all the different things I like.

**Thomas McDonnell (11)**
**Crumlin High School**


# Beautiful Birds

In the spring and summer
The birds fly around,
And as they fly, they make
A sweet, chirping sound.

It's lovely watching them
Sing and play all day,
And as darkness approaches,
They go on their way.

Their beautiful colours
Brighten up my day,
Every bird is unique
In its own special way.

**Jemma Greenberg (12)**
**Crumlin High School**

# Birds On The Roof

Little birds go *tweet, tweet, tweet,*
Aren't they oh so very sweet?
Feathers so soft and so dry,
As they let out their little cries.

Let it rain, oh let it rain,
So they can do their dance again,
They like to splish
They like to splash,
If it rained a mile away, you'd see them dash.

All of a sudden it begins to lash,
They flap so hard they almost crash,
I watch them splash
I watch them play,
They'd be the only ones happy, if it rained all day.

So I end this poem upon these roofs,
Watching these little birds, just act like goofs,
The friendliest birds I've ever met
And I've just realised, I'm getting wet.

**Luke Campbell  (11)**
**Crumlin High School**


# Myself

I am the child of my parents.
I love swimming.
I work hard at my drama classes.
I wish I was on holiday on my own.
I fear Daddy Long Legs.
I believe in a haunted house with ghosts.
I see Miss McCormick.
I hear the wind.
I eat beefburgers, beans, chips and red jelly.
I am David Ingram.

**David Ingram  (11)**
**Crumlin High School**

# Birds

Birds, birds, it's time to go
Just in case it starts to snow.
The colder it gets
The earlier the sun sets.
In case you get lost
Watch out for Jack Frost.
Your prey are all dying
So you will be crying.
So off you go to a warm, sunny land
Where there is lots of sea and sand.
When springtime is near
Everyone will cheer
Hooray, hooray, the birds are here!

**Liam Murphy (11)**
**Crumlin High School**


# My Name

E than is my name
T rying hard is my aim.
H appy, happy, happy, ho!
A nnoying my sister as I go,
N ice to see you, to see you nice.

S tunning that's what I'd call my life.
T ired, that's what I get at night,
E ven when I turn on my light.
W eetabix for my breakfast, never,
A lways Mum says will you ever? (eat it).
R eady, steady, here I go
T o my school (oh no!)

**Ethan Stewart (11)**
**Crumlin High School**

# About Me!

At home I love to play on my bike
My favourite make is Nike
One of my favourite colours is green
On my school tie, this can be seen.

At home I've got a dog called Brandy,
I know I shouldn't, but I feed her candy!
My favourite dinner is potatoes and meat,
I always find this a great treat.

The school I'm at is Crumlin High
Where I live is quite nearby.
The street I live in is Tromery Park
Where my dog likes to play and bark.

**Scott Adams (11)**
**Crumlin High School**


# My Name Poem

N is for Neil, which is my name.
E is for excitable, which I always am.
I is for interesting that I hope to be.
L is for loving that I can be.

B is for Ballinderry for where I live.
U is for useful that I can be.
T is for tense that I can get.
L is for lively that you can see.
E is for easy-going, a laid back kind of lad.
R is for right-handed which I am.

**Neil Butler (11)**
**Crumlin High School**

# My Name

J ack the Ripper is my nickname
A nd I really want to win the poetry game.
C ome along and play jacks with me,
K eep it up, 1, 2, 3.

D eegan is my second name,
E nergy is used for playing a game.
E veryone can play along,
G ames like sing a song.
A nd now you know my name is Jack,
N obody forget it, how about that!

**Jack Deegan  (11)**
**Crumlin High School**


# Myself

I am the child of my parents.
I love my parents.
I work at car washing.
I wish I could be a vet.
I fear dentists.
I believe that I am not dreaming.
I see the river in Switzerland.
I hear a noisy classroom.
I eat spaghetti Bolognese
I am what I am.
Who am I?
I am Elizabeth Churton.

**Elizabeth Churton  (11)**
**Crumlin High School**

# Myself

I am the child of my parents.
I love farming.
I work at history.
I wish I were 21.
I fear getting ill, I don't want to get cancer.
I believe I love my parents.
I see, I have seen half a cow.
I hear my teacher talking.
I like eating meat.
I am what I am.
Who am I?
Mark McBride.

**Mark McBride (11)**
**Crumlin High School**


# Myself

I am the child of my parents.
I love my parents.
I work at maths.
I wish to have a good life.
I fear the sea.
I believe my parents.
I see the big house on the beach.
I hear the birds.
I eat smoked salmon.
I am what I am.
Who am I?
Olya McCambridge.

**Olya McCambridge (13)**
**Crumlin High School**

# Myself

I am the child of my parents.
I love playing the PS2 and playing football.
I work at building model cars.
I wish I was in Australia.
I fear my mum shouting.
I believe science is a good subject.
I see a leisure pool.
I hear cars revving up.
I eat burgers and chips.
I am who I am.
I'm Ben Cormican.

**Ben Cormican (11)**
**Crumlin High School**


# Myself

I am the child of my parents.
I love trampolining.
I work at school.
I wish I was in Cork.
I fear spiders and rats.
I believe swimming keeps you fit.
I see Alison.
I hear a TV.
I eat burgers and chips.
I am Lucy Best.

**Lucy Best (11)**
**Crumlin High School**

# Myself

I am the child of my parents.
I love football, PS2, reading, skating.
I work hard at school.
I fear Arsenal or Chelsea winning the league.
I believe Man U and Rangers are the best.
I see that I am a very good swimmer and reader.
I hear the Formula 1 tune.
I wish that I could be a famous footballer or a Formula 1 racer.
I eat salad.
I am what I am.
I am Christopher Madden.

**Christopher Madden (11)**
**Crumlin High School**


# Myself

I am the child of my parents.
I love my mum and dad.
I work at cars.
I wish to be a millionaire.
I fear strangers and walking by myself at night.
I believe in football.
I see Ibrox.
I hear the Titanic.
I eat chips.
I am 11.
Who am I?
Ben Galloway.

**Ben Galloway (11)**
**Crumlin High School**

# Myself

I am the child of my parents.
I love my family.
I work at my school work.
I fear spiders.
I see Rangers winning the next match.
I wish I was in the USA.
I hear my favourite rock band called Green Day and NOFX
I eat pizza and chips.
I am what I am.
Who am I?
Ian Kirkland.

**Ian Kirkland (12)**
**Crumlin High School**


# Myself

I am the child of my parents.
I love farming.
I wish I didn't have to go to school.
I fear when I hear snakes nearby.
I believe I would make a good maths teacher.
I see the beach in Port Stewart.
I hear too much of Mrs Bell shouting at other people.
I eat steak.
I am what I am.
Who am I?
I'm Stuart Coulter.

**Stuart Coulter (12)**
**Crumlin High School**

# What Is Green?

Green are the leaves on the evergreen tree,
A greenfinch chirps as it flies past me.
The grass is growing beneath my feet,
I spot a toad, I was surprised to meet

Green is the kiwi fruit, round and sweet,
The lime and the apple, the grapes all a treat.
A cabbage, some broccoli and even peas,
'Eat up your greens,' exclaimed Mum, 'please!'

Green is the rain forest, moist and wet,
My project just finished, to be marked yet.
Plant life so varied and weather so hot,
The Kayapo people cooking manioc in a pot.

**Karl Taylor (11)**
**Crumlin High School**


# Myself

I am a child of my parents.
I love horses.
I work at horse riding.
I wish I had my own horse.
I fear cockroaches and scorpions.
I believe my parents are very nice.
I see Fantasy Island at Haven Golden Sands.
I hear my dad snoring.
I eat burger and chips.
I am what I am.
Who am I?
Jodie Cassidy.

**Jodie Cassidy (11)**
**Crumlin High School**

# Food Poem

S is for salmon that lives in the sea.
A is for apple that tastes good in a tart.
M is for melon that is yellow and big.
M is for mushroom that can be stuffed with garlic.
Y is for yoghurt that is made from milk.
J is for jam that can be spread on a scone.
O is for orange juice that quenches your thirst.

**Sammyjo Sloan (13)**
Cullybackey High School


# Food Poem

S is for strawberries that decorate a pavlova.
T is for turkey that is eaten at Christmas time.
A is for apples that are red, round and crunchy.
C is for chicken that tastes good in a curry.
E is for eggs that go *splat* on the plate.
Y is for yummy yoghurt that is made from cow's milk.

**Stacey Johnston (13)**
Cullybackey High School


# Food Poem

S is for soup that warms you up in winter.
T is for tart that is served with cream.
A is for apple that can be baked or stewed.
C is for carrot that can be used in a cake.
E is for egg that is oval in shape.
Y is for yoghurt that is creamy and light.

**Stacey McNeill (13)**
Cullybackey High School

# Orange

The welcoming candle flame invites you into the house.
A warm autumn day with a breeze in the air.
Leaves scurrying over the crisp, dry ground.
The sun setting on a hazy, warm summer's evening.
Goldfish swimming on the window sill.
Drinking Lucozade while laughing aloud.
All snuggled up in bed.

**Stacey Boardman (12)**
**Cullybackey High School**

# White

The polar bear runs through the falling snow
And slips upon the ice.
A bride walks up the aisle
Clutching a posy of snowdrops.
A herd of woolly sheep on their way
In search of Little Bo Peep.
The dove of peace soars up in the sky.

**Alison Simpson (12)**
**Cullybackey High School**

# Food Poem

G is for grapes that are bitter and sweet.
A is for apple that is red and round.
V is for veal that is tender to eat.
I is for ice cream that is sweet and cool.
N is for nuts that are hard to squash.

**Gavin Steele (13)**
**Cullybackey High School**

# Red

The heat of the sun on a warm summer's day.
The stop sign on a set of traffic lights.
The colour of blood oozing out of a fresh cut.
The red rose on Valentine's Day.
Your cheeks when you blush.
The warm fire flame on a cold winter's night.

**Melissa McCollum  (13)**
Cullybackey High School

# Red

Another day has come
The sun is staring me in the face
It's summer!
Everyone is sunburnt.
A fire engine flies by
There's blood on the road
Splatters on the black tar.

**Lee Wilson  (12)**
Cullybackey High School

# Green

The grass on a newly cut lawn.
Trees bent in a forest after a gale.
A little budgie chirping loudly.
A swarm of horseflies circling dung.
A poor sailor's face on a stormy sea.

**William McIntosh  (13)**
Cullybackey High School

# Green

Spring buds push into the
Pale sunlight and develop into leaves.
Grassy banks which put a spring in your step.
Frogs jump for joy in slimy swamps
And hop to a safe lily pad.

**Helen Shaw (12)**
Cullybackey High School


# Food

M ark is for mushy peas that can slide down your throat,
A is for apples so red and so round,
R is for raspberries, eaten with ice cream.
K is for KitKat when having a break.

**Mark Kilpatrick (13)**
Cullybackey High School


# Prague

To make Prague you need lots of:

Good places to go,
Very cold winters
Nice warm summers
An astronomical clock

Rich, fancy hotels
Famous bridges and rivers
Very tall mountains
Tall, straight-faced guards at the palace
Tours around the town
Lots of amber jewellery
And beautiful coloured glass

Cook in an oven for one hour and guess what?
Prague.

**Dearbhlagh Moore (12)**
Dominican College

# In The Eyes Of A Stranger

Ireland is so beautiful, like an open door it has many possibilities,
There may be streams to the left and green pastures to the right,
But it always feels like home, no matter where you're from.

In Spain there is sun, the most glorious of all,
See shadows dancing on the garden wall.
You could stay outside for days, just soaking up the rays.

In France, in France there is shopping galore,
From food to pets, that is what France is for.
Cafés here, boutiques there, shops and
Shopping everywhere.

Belgium so sweet, home of all the chocolate I could eat,
Where so many languages are told and the people grow so old.
Maybe it's the food they eat, like chocolate-covered, chewy feet.

Russia, it's the trip of a lifetime, but don't forget your scarf
and gloves,
When you look at the snow mountains they disappear,
But be sure that they're always there, just so beautiful
That you can't see them.

I was a stranger to this land, a trip once most daunting,
But now I think, 'Why, it's Europe!'

**Claire Mullan** (13)
**Dominican College**

# Europe Has Its Differences But We Are All The Same!

Some people are from England,
Some people are from Spain;
But every single one of them
Really hates the rain.

Some people are black,
Some people are yellow,
But you can put a smile on their face
By just saying, 'Hello.'

Some people are from Ireland,
Some people are from France,
But what's the difference anyway?
We all wear underpants.

Some people believe in nothing,
Some people have faith,
But we all would do anything
To keep our children safe.

Some cultures are Chinese,
Some cultures are Thai,
But everyone in Europe
Lives under the same sky.

**Annaliese McCrisken  (13)**
**Dominican College**

# My Magical Kingdom

Europe, Europe, what a wonderful sight,
The feeling of being so small, but being in something so big.
Fascination, the attraction, the delight,
The dreams that I dream of what Europe will be.

America, the king of the world,
Although not in Europe, it still rules them all.
Like the king of his castle, looking down at the world as his kingdom,
Yes, America rules them all.

My dreams take me to it on a magical journey every night.
As I look down over the country, like a bird in flight,
I look down at the lights,
It's my magical kingdom now.

New York, New York,
The city that never sleeps.
But it has to sleep sometime doesn't it?
And when it does you can only hear the gentle sound of the wind.

The people are busy; they are all one big family,
Like ants of a colony, helping each other.
In winter the city lies like a still river,
But if you start it up, a ripple begins its life.

So small at first, but then look how it grows,
But someone has to start them, the people of New York.

The shops of the city, the gleaming windows,
The smell of money when you enter, and the road rage when
you appear.
The roads are little dots of yellow throughout the city,
They drive through the city like the dots on a polka dot dress.

Yes, yes, New York is the place for me,
In my mind it is the magical kingdom waiting to be explored.

**Hayley Russell  (13)**
**Dominican College**

# I'm Fine Where I Am!

I'm fine where I am.
Russia is cold and everyone looks old.
In Scandinavia they all blabba a lot of ABBA!
In France it's snails and frogs washed down with wine,
It's not how I like to dine!
Spain has little or no rain and the waiters are a pain!
Portugal they drink sherry and are very merry!
In Italy they eat garlic, basil and dill,
As a result their breath is not brill.
Greece, it's very hot and it makes the earth quake a lot.
Switzerland and Austria are land-locked and with
Mountains so high, the view is blocked.

It's green, the people aren't mean, the food is good
You're sure to come back because of the craic
Better than the rest, good old Ireland is the best.

**Jessica Turner  (13)**
**Dominican College**


# Europe

Europe is a place of interest,
Sights and sounds to see and hear,
Different cultures, different people,
All living on one country shared.

One day I hope I will go to France
And see the famous Eiffel Tower,
To sail long the canals
And just relax for a couple of hours.

But at the moment I'm where I belong,
In Ireland where I'm content,
As I live among my family and friends
And where my life so far has been spent.

**Sarah Cochrane  (14)**
**Dominican College**

# Fading Reflection

Every day I feel that I don't belong,
I constantly wonder, have I done something wrong?
My parents ignore me and give no guidance at all,
When I try talking to them, it's like they are a brick wall.

Praise me, shout at me, show any emotion,
They look at me blankly, they haven't a notion.
They don't understand me, they don't see my pain,
I spend so much time alone, I wonder if I'm sane.

At school I'm an outcast, I don't fit in.
Me being myself, is it really a sin?
My peers tease and taunt me, wanting to see me cry,
I pretend to not hear them, my head held high.

Inside I am crying, but this falls on deaf ears,
I won't let anyone see my eyes brimmed with tears.
I can't let them know that they have scarred me deep down,
At their jeering I give them only a frown.

I am slowly disappearing and soon I shall be gone,
Equality for everyone must be a con,
Because if it were so, then why has my life been this way?
Soon I'll just be another distant memory of yesterday.

**Maeve Corrigan (14)**
**Dominican College**

# Silence

I look around and I do see some beautiful and wondrous things
I can smell my hair and I can smell the sea
I can feel the grass damp and ticklish upon my feet

But I hear no voices and I hear no music
No one listens and no one cares
I cannot explain to them my despair

I cannot read
I cannot write
To learn you need more than sight
I've tried before but I am weak
I've lost the will to learn to speak

Why did you send me here?
I've often thought through my tears
I've never laughed
I've never smiled
Isolated as a child

I've never been ill
But pain I feel
I am weary and frustrated
This is the life that I've been given
Doomed to eternal silence
Separated from the living.

**Rachel MacDonald  (14)**
**Dominican College**

# Autumn

Look at the trees everywhere,
The branches are nearly all bare.
The leaves are spiralling, twirling down,
They come with a crash, thud to the ground.

Everyone is cuddling by the fire,
The wind is strong and often dire.
The trees are blowing from side to side,
And the rain begins to glide.

Children outside jump into the leaves,
People are coughing and begin to sneeze.
Girls play conkers,
While the boys go bonkers, playing in the trees.

The birds swoop down and lie around
But the scarecrows scare them off,
So away they fly
And chirp off into the sky.

**Louise Armstrong  (14)**
**Dominican College**

# What Being A European Means!

Being a European,
It means nothing to me.
I wish I lived in France,
With all the sights to see!

French people are so nice there,
Their language is most interesting.
The Eiffel Tower, the Arc de Triomphe,
The galleries full of paintings.

One day I will live there
And see all those beautiful sights.
But for now, I'm in Northern Ireland,
A European in Northern Ireland.

**Roslyn Cooke  (13)**
**Dominican College**

# Funny Thing Love Is

Funny thing love is.
Like a rampant disease
She inflames the mind, numbs the senses,
Making the affected person lose all sense of reality.

Funny thing love is.
When people are willing
To fight for her, die for her,
Probably just to say that they have known her touch.

Funny thing love is.
She has consequences that
Can create pain, can create hurt.
Condemning a person to a lifetime of despair and loneliness.

Funny thing love is.
Even when her wrath is unleashed,
People never lose hope, lose faith.
Leading us to believe that she is worth it all.

**Mary McCaughey  (18)**
**Dominican College**


# One Nation

In Europe we have a future
For everyone of different culture.
So many different nationalities
All of those interesting personalities.

Almost every place I go
I can now spend the Euro.
But we still have many different languages
Across the large family of diverse races.

We will soon just be one big country,
But will they learn to make an Ulster fry?
Because I want to feel at home
In Vienna, Paris, Madrid, Berlin or Rome.

**Emma Wilson  (14)**
**Dominican College**

# Europe, Half Hot, Half Cold!

When Mum exclaimed, 'We're off to sunny Spain!'
My first thought was, naturally, *finally, away from the rain*'
I bought loads of stylish gear.
It was Mum's cheque book, no fear.
I packed my case and to the airport we went.
From the car park to the door I was totally drenched.
So, I said to Dad, 'This weather's so sad! I'll be soaking up the sun
While they'll be trapped, like in 'Chicken Run'.'

Once, when we got off the plane,
I suddenly screamed, 'I'm in Spain!'

The people there were far too square,
So I said they need to let down their hair!
I showed them how to party,
So they'd be super happy!
I took them clubbing
Which they were loving!

But a fortnight passed,
My time didn't last,
So I was shifted back home
To listen to the newsreader's drone,
Informing us who petrol-bombed who,
As if they even have a clue.

Being a European means much to me,
As long as I'm in a different country,
Especially one that's humid and hot,
So I'll love Europe a whole lot!

**Sarah Faloon (11)**
**Dominican College**

# In Ballycastle Oh!

We get into the car
And in over an hour
We arrive in Ballycastle
Where our caravan is and all of our friends
And nothing is too much hassle.

If the sun is shining, we go to the beach,
Our bodyboards, towels and cream.
It's just down the hill, it's handy to reach,
We stay hours, it's truly a dream.

When the sun goes down and it starts to get dark
All the families gather to eat.
The barbecues are lit, children play in the park,
Each time it's really a treat.

Dad gets his guitar and the singsong starts
Everyone takes it in turn.
We sing and laugh all the songs from the charts
While the barbecues continue to burn.

All of the summer and weekends too
In Ballycastle we can be found,
Fishing, walking, having fun all day through,
It's the best place I know, yes it's sound.

**Aíne Rogan  (11)**
**Dominican College**

# Exploring Europe

Belfast, Belfast, such a beautiful town,
But not as beautiful as County Down.
Belfast, Belfast, I love you
And because you are in Ireland too.

One day I took a trip to Dublin town,
Stayed there for a few days,
Hoping my skin would turn brown.
Moved on for a few days to Donegal,
Where I met a nice man
And his name was Paul.

Went to the docks
And caught a boat from there,
Ended up in Scotland
And then drove to Blackpool fair.
It was a very long while,
But it was worth the wait
And it was worth it when I saw my mates.

The next year I went to Spain and Malta too,
I saw all the sights, parks and zoos.

Came back home from holidays on 8th June,
I went to give out some presents,
But Mum said, 'Not so soon.'

So that ends my journey of my few days away.
But not to worry, I'll be back some day.

**Kerri-Louise Murray (11)**
**Dominican College**

# Home Sweet Home

Let me tell you a bit about myself,
My favourite team,
There is only one.
The Celtic boys are on the run!
They are fit and gorgeous
And Larsson's mine, so hands off.
My favourite place is 'home sweet home',
Ireland, it might not be warm,
But it's still great.
The people are friendly
And shopping in Dublin is second to none!
My favourite colours are lilac and pink,
I love them to pieces,
Pink, pink, pink!

My favourite band was S Club 7,
I was so sad when they broke up!
They had the best songs ever.
I just loved Bradley,
I went to the Odessy
To see them sing, dance and do their thing.
My favourite food is sweet and sour chicken,
I gobble it up,
And my dog sits hoping for a little bit,
But I say no, it's too nice to give away!
I love wearing jeans and skirts,
Strappy tops or lovely designer ones,
But sometimes I want too much!

**Mary McGurk (12)**
**Dominican College**

# Europe

In Europe there are many different countries,
There are about 250,000,000 people in all,
The Euro has just been introduced,
And it's not ready to fall.

Although they are all one continent,
Spain, France, UK,
Germany, Italy, Austria and Hungary,
They all wanted it their own way!

I haven't seen it all,
I probably never will,
But all that I have seen of Europe,
It definitely has been brill.

When I was in Spain,
The sun, the sea and the sand,
And the bull fighting
And the rest of the land.

In France, the cuisine,
It really is the best.
Nothing can compare to it,
Even the best of the rest.

I've always lived in Ireland,
Every year of my life,
The green is always there,
Even when people are in strife.

I have been to many countries,
But some I have not.
Some were cold,
But lots were hot.

All the ones that I have seen
And all the ones I will,
I'm very glad to be European,
It has and will be a thrill!

**Nuala Meehan (14)**
**Dominican College**

# Europe Is The Best

Europe is the best
Better than all the rest.
Sun or hail or rain or snow,
Europe is the best, so here I go:

Spain and France and Italy,
They even give out a three-course meal.
Europe is a really big place to me,
There's lots of sights for you to see.

I'd love to go and visit France
And hopefully I would have a chance
To see the sights and Eiffel Tower,
And even taste their chocolate bars.

I'd love for you to come and see
The wonderful sights there can be.
I think Europe is best,
Better than all the rest.

**Nuala Stewart (11)**
**Dominican College**


# Sunday Morning St Johann

Sunday morning St Johann
I see ten or eleven women sitting outside
On a hot July day,
Sipping their wine, taking their time.

Their happiness puts me at ease
As they answer, 'Ja, bitte,'
To tourists who stutter over their phrase books,
'Kann ich dich fotografieren?'

I first saw them at half-nine mass.
Golden angels gazed down on them
As the golden tassels bobbled from their black top hats.
They looked at home in the baroque church,
Both cherished memories of Europe's past.

**Bríd McGuinness (13)**
**Dominican College**

# Europe And Me!

Being European
Doesn't mean much to me,
Sometimes you just ignore
What you cannot see.

The European Union
Was set up for peace,
From Austria to Italy
And Portugal to Greece.

There are 47 countries in Europe,
I'd like to visit them all,
From Russia which is the biggest,
To the Vatican which is quite small.

Ireland's the country I'm from,
And the country I love the most.
Wherever I go in Europe,
I won't be ashamed to boast!

**Theresa Shields (13)**
**Dominican College**


# My Hedgehog Wish

I wish I was a hedgehog, sleeping in the leaves,
It is the start of hibernation
Underneath those frosty trees,
With my needle-sharp back and my wet and shiny nose,
My small beady eyes and toothpick little toes.

A gardener's friend, I come to lunch,
Juicy slugs and bugs I munch,
Underneath the stones and leaves
I can eat as much as I please.

So for all the hedgehogs throughout the land,
Stay curled up as tight as you can.

**Niamh McCallin (14)**
**Dominican College**

# Autumn

Time to gather in the sheaves.
Corn, wheat, apples on trees.
The nights are long, the days are short,
Time to strengthen every fort.

Autumn colours fill the earth,
A coal fire, a warm hearth.
Conkers, chestnuts, sycamore planes,
The damp smell of autumn rains.

Berries, twigs and brown-red leaves,
Float to the ground in the autumn breeze.
Birds and insects search the lawn,
Preparing nests for winter's grey dawn.

But cold to come and colder still,
With harsh, sharp winds to bend our will.
Soon winter will show her grey, bleak face,
But onwards to spring and the seasonal race.

**Sharon Mullan (18)**
**Dominican College**


# What Will This World Become?

What will this world become?
Will we keep having to hide our religion from some
In fear of what they do or say
To hurt us in any way?

Over the years, violence has got worse,
Families have buried loved ones who were
Victims of the troubles.
Will another life have to be lost, and
More families left to pay the cost,
Before people decide to get on with their lives
And put away for good their bombs, guns and knives?

**Kathleen McCoey**
**Dominican College**

# My Journey To School In The Autumn

My journey to school begins the moment I walk out the door.
I amble up the cracked concrete path that leads
To the rusty green gate
Which is stuck most of the time and cannot be opened
Without using force.
I give it a hard kick, it screeches open and I traipse out
With all my bags onto the street
Darkened by trees which grow every twenty feet or so.

The sky as we approach winter, is much more benighted
And is full of grey nimbi.
As I trudge my way through the piles of crisp autumn leaves,
More are pirouetting down from the branches
High above my head.
The golden leaves crunch underfoot and the icy wind
Cuts through me.
I can hear the rumble of traffic in the distance,
And the birds twittering around me.

I reach the crossroads and, as there are no cars approaching,
I stride carefully and purposefully across the vacant road.
As I reach the other side, I see Amber, my uncle's guide dog
Bounding towards me, full of energy
And he saunters along happily by my side.
When we reach his house, he leaps into the car boot,
Ready for another working day.

When everyone is ready and waiting in the car,
We drive through the neighbourhood
Until we reach the main road and get stuck
In huge, hectic traffic jams (every morning)
As I sit on the back seat, stationary,
I watch the world revolving around outside.
There are children on buses, frustrated adults in cars
And people walking without a care.
We beat through the traffic and I get dropped off
At the great, blue-grey school gates.

I casually stroll up the dark, wide, spooky path
Towards the newly built school building.
The school grounds are more or less deserted as I am here early
And some pupils are at home or still in their beds,
But most will be on their way to school.
I summon all my energy to climb the flights and flights
Of blue stairs to my classroom
And by the time I get there, I feel like I could go to bed for a month!

**Claire Glover  (14)**
**Dominican College**

# Detention

In my school there's lots of rules
Whether you like it or not!
And if you don't obey them,
Detention's what you've got.

Detention is so boring,
All I have is lines.
I wish I had obeyed the rules,
But now I'm 'doing time'.

I should have done my homework,
I was just being lazy,
If I get detention again,
It'll drive me crazy.

Detention is a punishment
You get when you break the rules,
You miss after school activity
Because you played the fool.

**Aoife Kelly  (14)**
**Dominican College**

# The Festival

Sitting on your chair, restlessly anticipating
Outwardly applauding your competitors
Inwardly cursing their talented fingers
Wondering why on earth you entered
When you haven't got a hope in hell.

Barely hearing your name called
Rising, you know your fate lies ahead
Somewhere concealed under the ivory keys
Lurking deep within the mahogany case
Waiting for its release.

You arrange yourself demurely on the stool
Trying to appear as the professional
You desperately wish you were
As your stomach squirms itself into a pretzel
You wait for the pompous judges' nod.

You position your fingers hesitantly over the keys
Wondering where your polished fingernails disappeared
Taking a deep breath of the humid hall's air
To stop the nervous shaking your body has surrendered to
Then, miraculously, with ease and confidence you begin to play.

**Catherine McCann  (14)**
**Dominican College**

# Light

We turn on a light
So that we can see.
A light can mean hope,
It can mean you are free.
A light can bring comfort
From darkness and fear.
A light for the way
Can make everything clear.
But sometimes, no matter
How light it can be,
A light's not enough
To make everyone see.
Sometimes the light's
Shining right in your eyes,
But you choose to ignore,
To pretend, to disguise.
There will always be darkness
And fear and regret,
If we close our eyes
And choose to forget.
When you hide behind excuses,
When you close your mind,
How can you see
If you choose to be blind?

**Aine Gallagher (15)**
**Dominican College**

# Masquerade

A twirl of colour,
enrapturing delight,
a midnight feast
of masks at night!
Where one and all
can come and hide,
their faults, their fears,
their face, their lies.
And even after their carousel is done,
and the stars fade away,
and out comes the sun,
they shall wear their masks
through dawn till dusk,
leading their lives of power, lust,
greed, and mistrust.

**Laura Robinson** **(13)**
**Dominican College**


# Hallowe'en

Monkey nuts, pumpkins, apple tarts too,
Fun games and party tricks all the night through.

Dressing up spookily, knocking on doors,
The night's still young, let's grab some more!

Tonight is the night of the living dead,
Skeletons, zombies, and men with no heads.

Fireworks going off all through the night,
Exploding so suddenly, giving us a fright.

It's cold and windy and I'm getting a chill,
Thinking about tonight . . . oh, such a thrill!

Ghouls and ghosts and witches and all,
Can't wait for tonight, we'll all have a ball!

**Lauren O'Hagan** **(13)**
**Dominican College**

# What Do You See, Teacher?

What do you see, teacher?
What do you see?
What are you thinking when
You are looking at me?

Do you see a small child,
Unhappy and sad,
With no friends,
A mum or a dad

Who stares out of the window
In the very back row,
Who doesn't care about maths
Or English you know?

Is this what you see, teacher?
Is this what you see?
Is this what you are thinking when
You are looking at me?

If it is, teacher,
Look closer,
Look closer, see . . . me.

**Órla Morrow  (13)**
**Dominican College**

# The Winds Of Europe

The winds of Europe come from every direction,
For me to taste and smell.
First comes the reek of dampened grass of home,
That I know so well.

The cold winds from Scandinavia
Are full of the tangy scent of pine
And French breezes brim with baking bread
And long-fermented wine.

From Austria and Germany comes
Fresh mountain air,
Mixed with the bitter taste of 'kaffee'
Hot and ready to share.

Great Britain: London air hums
With people, cities, smoke and smog
And Iceland smells of hot springs
And fire-burning log.

Spanish air pulses with flamenco
Music, life and song.
Italy is an opera of pasta, olives,
And tomatoes in the sun too long.

This is Europe
This is what it means to me
A melting pot of peoples
Of cultural diversity.

**Christina Neill (13)**
**Dominican College**

# Tiger

The tiger is a cunning cat; his coat is smooth and sleek,
So should he be a living room mat,
Or in a circus, timid and weak?

The tiger is a fearsome king; have you ever heard him roar?
He belongs in a jungle, where birds fly and sing,
Not lying on a cold cage floor.

But he's been locked in a dark, dreary cell at the annual county fair,
Why was this happening? He couldn't tell
And no one seemed to care.

Homesick, blue and especially cold, angry and full of sorrow,
His sad eyes have lost their glint of gold,
His life will only be worse tomorrow.

What *is* the point of owning a life that's not your own?
Locked up in a cage, groaning,
When really you belong on a throne?

In life this tiger won't go far, it's a rumour but has been said,
The famous circus just lost their star,
Their main attraction's . . .
Dead.

**Helen McDermott  (13)**
**Dominican College**

# School Life

I would just like to tell you what my life is like,
I've got a lot to say about me and my school life.
Sometimes I feel it's just too much,
Others I just seem to be enjoying the work.

KS3 exams stand before me,
Like something out of a ghoulish nightmare,
Although we do get lots of help with our maths, English and science,
Some subjects just seem to drag on.

I love some subjects, languages especially.
But drama and IT are brilliant as well.
And all of them are taught in lovely rooms, regardless of where
they are.
We've got a lovely new building, which I will just tell you about now.

Dozens of rooms, corridors so long,
They are so spacious, yet so thin.
Beautifully decorated by the teachers that use them.
The top floor is the lightest in colour - a lovely, breathtaking blue,
so light.

**Grace Hughes  (13)**
**Dominican College**

# My Sanctuary

My sanctuary, you cannot see.
My sanctuary, you cannot feel.
My sanctuary, you can only hear,
But it envelops me so much
That I can see it, feel it,
Hear it, sense it in every way.

What is my sanctuary? It is music.

The beat of the drums,
The rumble of the bass,
The twang of the guitar,
Entrances me and takes me
To faraway lands
Where troubles don't matter,
Where enemies don't exist.

If only you could enter
My sanctuary,
My life,
My soul.

**Aisling Thompson  (14)**
**Dominican College**

# Hallowe'en

Hallowe'en to me means
Fireworks, bright skies,
I love to watch the people in the street
In their costumes.
Some young, some old.

Hallowe'en to me means
Party time, but also family.
As I rush about getting ready
I hear the car doors bang and a rap on the door.
I know who it is:
*My family.*

While the fun and games start,
My dad brings my cousins and me out
Hallowe'en rhyming, when we return,
We know everyone will be waiting for us.

**Orla Corey  (13)**
**Dominican College**


# Autumn

Autumn is the season of dullness and grey,
Most people go through it day by day.
Autumn is when the leaves go red and green,
It is the season of fallen leaves, not a beautiful scene.

Autumn is after the season of warmth to fulfil,
Autumn is before the season of giving and goodwill.
Autumn is the season of nature and darkness,
Autumn is the season of wind and coolness.

Autumn is when you stand on the leaves
And hear the crunching and crumble and heave.
Autumn is the time that you dress up and spook.
Autumn is my favourite season.

**Oonagh McVeigh  (13)**
**Dominican College**

# The Séance

She gazes into the orb's crystalline depths,
All in the room are holding their breath.
Her eyes are glinting, like emeralds are winking,
As if she knows something we do not.

As she chants, surrounded by burning candles,
The air smells sour
'Tis the witching hour and nothing is the same.

Throughout the woods, the wind rides out,
Whilst the lightning flashes
And the thunder crashes.
You can hear the rain beating against
The sleepy-looking oak trunks.

Back in the cave
There is a sharp intake of breath
As she asks the spirits to rise.

In the flickering candlelight
The temperature drops,
Everyone feels the happiness floating out of the room.

You can smell the blood,
The death, the despair.
In the pale moonlight, the spirit rises, floating, screaming,
No one helped her when she was dying,
No one helped her . . . would you?

**Anne Crummey  (13)**
**Dominican College**

# Why?

I am only 12, there's not much I can do.
I can handle studies and homework,
I want there to be world peace and equality too.
I am only 12, there's not much I can do.

Why are there wars?
And fighting, that is wrong.
I don't understand,
But I'm sure it won't take me long!
I don't have to think twice
To know what you're doing is bad.
Don't you know there's children all over this planet
That you're making sad?

Why is there pollution?
Big factories letting off smoke,
You don't know what you're doing!
Look out of the window and up into the sky.
It's blue, with clouds and birds flying so high.
One day we won't have it, won't have it at all,
And there won't be anyone to blame,
Or to take the fall.

I am only 12, there's not much I can do.
Black, white, fat or thin,
We all share the same world that we live in.
We are people and that is true,
We all should be treated like me and you.
I am only 12, there's not much I can do.

**Joanne Connor (12)**
**Dominican College**

# I Will Never Forget You

It has been so long since I have talked to you.
The days seem like years, and yet there are so few.
I remember the good days when you laid me down and sang
                                      me to sleep
The tunes you sang so soft and sweet are here with me still.

I remember the times when I was bad,
You shouted at me and made me sad,
But that's OK Mummy, I forgive you now,
You're in a better place now, but I don't know how.

Why did you go Mummy? I wanted so much for you to stay.
Was it because I was bad Mummy? If it was, I am sorry.
Was it my fault Mummy? I didn't mean to make you cry
When I said I missed Daddy and you didn't seem to care.

Can you see him Mummy? Tell him I said hi.
My tummy hurts Mummy, I'll try not to cry.
But I miss you so much Mummy, it hurts me inside.
I wish you would come home, for I don't want to hide.

Do you miss me Mummy? Because I miss you too.
I love you Mummy, do you love me too?
I wish that one day I could visit you in Heaven,
OK, I'll sleep with the light on in case you come home
And kiss me goodnight. I miss you Mummy.

**Lorna Benson  (14)**
**Dominican College**

# Why?

Across the peace lines, over the divides
Sectarian hatred we all can't hide
Prejudice a big killer, hatred is shown
Peace in Northern Ireland we have never known
Terrorists' hearts filled up with hate
We can make a change; it's never too late
Open your yes and look all around
Protestants with Catholics will never be found
It doesn't have to stay this way
Let's make a stand, change it all today
We can join together, unite as one
Our battle for peace might just be won
Over the barricades, across the divides
A solution to the trouble we strain to find
Loyalists and republicans can't pass each other
Why can't we all just get on with each other?
Children often bear the brunt of it all
All the violence has no call
Across the peace lines, over the divides
Sectarian hatred we all can't hide.

**Lisa Dwyer  (14)**
**Dominican College**

# The Hedgehog

As I was walking along the road,
What did I see,
But a little funny face
Looking up at me!

As I walked a little closer
Its face was very small,
It got a little scared
And curled up into a spiked ball.

As I picked it up,
It had a tiny, button nose
And beady little eyes,
And curly little toes.

As I set the hedgehog down,
He scurried into the grass
As he looked around for his food.
Forever this memory will last.

**Seánna O'Neill  (13)**
**Dominican College**


# Autumn

Look at the leaves floating in the breeze,
Twisting, turning, dancing in the lonely midnight breeze,
Give a little twirl,
Give a little twist,
Give a little loop,
And now salute.
Look at the leaves,
Look at the trees,
There are no more leaves left on the trees.

**Eryn Purdy  (11)**
**Dunclug College**

# Winter Is Coming

Winter is coming and everyone knows it,
It will bring fun and joy,
With children playing in fields of snow,
How much more joy could it bring?

When it comes, snowmen will be everywhere,
Cold snow will melt and vanish,
So play as much as you can,
Because it doesn't last all year.

You can do anything you want,
But don't overdo it or none will be left,
So plenty of snow will be left,
Now you can watch it melt
And wait till next year until it comes back.

**Christopher Blair  (12)**
**Dunclug College**


# Children

Children playing with their toys,
There is hardly any noise,
Everyone gives a big sigh,
All they hear is the train going by.

In the coolness of the night,
Lit only by moonlight,
People run along the streets
As the children sit in their seats.

The curtains are closed, it's time for bed,
It's time to rest that weary head.
Now go to sleep,
Without a peep.

**Alan Thompson  (12)**
**Dunclug College**

# Cats

Some cats are so fluffy
And they love getting scruffy!
Their eyes are so green
It makes them look mean.

They miaow, not bark.
They can see in the dark.
They go hunting at night
And come home at daylight.

When they look for their food
They want it to be good,
The food they think is nice,
Are big, juicy mice!

So lovely as kittens,
You can easily be smitten.
They are company for wives,
They've even nine lives.

**Ashley Kernohan (12)**
**Dunclug College**

# Horses

Horses running wild,
Horses running free.
Horses galloping,
Trotting, even walking.

The moon twinkling above
With the stars.
Horses talking with the stars,
Sky and moon.

**Phillip Tynan (12)**
**Dunclug College**

# My Hamster, Always Remembered

My hamster was called Pickles,
My mum always shouted, 'Hamsters are banned!'
I put little Pickles in her hands and pleaded,
'Go on Mum, it tickles.'
Then she muttered, 'Keep her, she's grand.'

I played with her until it was late,
When I tried to get away from her, she looked at me
As if to say, 'No way, kid.'
If she saw a cat and you looked in her eyes,
You could notice the hate.
I though to myself, *If I put her up for sale,*
*We'd get a pretty high bid.*

*But one day we had to take her to the vet!*

The vet said, 'Sorry son, have to put her to sleep.'
All I could say was, 'Why me?'
I was crying hard and my breathing was deep.
Why, oh why did we have to put her to sleep?

But Pickles is always remembered,
And she is now sleeping peacefully at the bottom of my garden
Under a holly tree, at rest.

**Aaron McCormack  (12)**
**Dunclug College**


# School Is Over

School is at an end,
I run with my friend
To the sports shop
To buy a top,
Then we go to the bus
And then we start a fuss.
I get home and start to play.
'Where have you been?' Mum would say.

**Andrew McIlmoyle & Gareth Dunwoody  (11)**
**Dunclug College**

# To The Crazy Ones

Here's to the crazy ones,
The misfits, the rebels,
The troublemakers.

The ones who see things differently,
They're not fond of rules.
You can praise them, disagree with them,
Quote them, disbelieve them,
Or just think they're plain thick,
But the only thing you can't do with them is ignore them.

You'll see them on the Kerrang! channel,
The school and even the most normal and social of places.
I am not saying that the monkey stuff is true,
But people do evolve and change.

The crazy ones push the human race forward.
Maybe they have to be crazy.
How else can you stare at a picture full of muddled up faces
And see a work of art,
Or sit in silence and hear a song that has never been written?
Or gaze into the night sky and see little green men
Flying about, ready to invade Earth?
While some see them as crazy ones, some people see geniuses,
Because the people who are crazy enough to think
They can change the world,
Are the ones that do.

**Nigel McMullen (12)**
**Dunclug College**

# The Seal Haiku

A seal lays tired
It falls asleep on the beach
And then stays the night

**Mark Kennedy (11)**
**Dunclug College**

# My Family

My family are sometimes happy,
Not when sad or yappy,

When angry they get
So mad and sometimes bad,

They shout when they
Can't hear the telly,

They are mostly nice,
But never as quiet as mice.

My dad is very sleepy,
But can be very sneaky.

The rest of them
Are truly annoying,

But whatever way,
I still love them every single day.

**Debbie McDowell (12)**
**Dunclug College**


# My Nutter Dog

I have a dog who's a bit of a nutter.
He sometimes chases birds, who give a little flutter.
He plays with his ball
And sometimes falls.
And at night when he's asleep,
The little fleas begin to creep.
Scratch, scratch, scratch,
As he opens the little latch
And out he comes with a bit of a clutter,
Once again the little birds begin to flutter.

**Lyndsay McPhee (12)**
**Dunclug College**

# Dogs

Dogs go anywhere, uphill and down
Across the countryside or to the town
They go out with their fur clean
And come back creating a scene!
They bark by day and bark by night
Some children get a really big fright
The neighbours shout
When the dogs are about,
We ask, 'What'll we do, throw them out?'
They make a mess . . .
Argh! My mum's so stressed
They always need their food.
Why can't they be good?
And when you play,
They *never* obey!
They say a dog's a man's best friend,
Well, they drive me round the bend
They don't wear clothes,
Well they're dogs I suppose.
I'd better go,
The dog's eating my toe.
Argh!

**Rachael Frew  (12)**
**Dunclug College**


# My Granny

G one are the days when you were young,

R unning, playing and having fun.

A lthough your hair is turning grey,

N o one cares, I love you anyway. You

N ever forget my birthday, although I would not mind,

Y ou know I think you're adorable, proud, strong and kind.

**Sarah Rusk  (12)**
**Dunclug College**

# Seasons

Leaves begin to fall off the trees,
Before the winter comes in with a breeze,
Brushing and blowing all over the grass,
Watched by the people that pass.

Summer has come with a shine,
Children come out with a bang.
The summer is over, now we must go,
Summer has left us with a shine.

Autumn has come with a chill,
Now we must take a pill.
Winter is in,
It's time to go.

**David Chesney & Daniel McClean (11)**
**Dunclug College**

# The Sun And The Moon

I look to the west and see the sun,
I look to the east and see the moon.
Are they the same, they both give light?
One rules the day
And one rules the night.

**Thomas McGuigan (12)**
**Dunclug College**

# Wintertime! Haiku

Freezing cold weather,
Snowflakes falling all around,
Snowmen being built.

**Kara Thompson (12)**
**Dunclug College**

# Glasgow Rangers

Glasgow Rangers are the best,
Everyone knows they're better than the rest.
Last season they won the treble,
They are absolutely lethal!
They have won the league 50 times,
But to become the best in Europe, that will take time.
Rangers are the title holders,
And I will still support them when I'm older.

**Ryan Wilson (13)**
**Dunclug College**

# Monkeys

Swinging way up in the treetops,
Way up in the sky,
That's where you see them swing,
Up on high.

Tempt them with bananas,
Tempt them with fruit,
They will appear from everywhere,
From the treetops to the roots.

**Adam Rodgers (12)**
**Dunclug College**

# Bunnies Haiku

Big lovely soft tail
Hops about the long green grass
I love bunnies so.

**Jade McAuley (11)**
**Dunclug College**

# Wishes

When I'm sad,
When I'm lonely,
Put on some music,
This won't make me mad.

Pictures in a locket
Bringing me some smiles,
Making me really happy . . .
By putting money in my pocket.

Buy me a sports car,
I can learn to drive.
By shutting my wee brother up
I'll buy you a chocolate bar.

Buy me some new clothes,
I will look really good,
To keep the world dressed in
The finest robes.

**Susan Smyth  (12)**
**Dunclug College**

# Black Panther Haiku

Panthers are silent
Hidden in the long dark grass
All are very fast.

**Simon Herbison  (11)**
**Dunclug College**

# My Haiku

Christmas is here now
Snow is falling all around
Time to celebrate!

**Emma Leonard  (11)**
**Dunclug College**

# Dogs

Dogs are my favourite animals, puppies too,
Any kind of do will do.
I just love them all,
Fat, skinny, big or small, they are all so cute.
Not all dogs are nice.
If you are nice, they will be too.
There are lots of different types,
But I love them all.
I just can't help myself when I see one hurt,
I just have to cry.
I have one of my own,
Pippa is her name.
She is a golden retriever,
Also, she too is a babe.
She will always be too.
That is just my opinion,
So now tell me yours.

**Natalia McConnell  (11)**
**Orangefield High School**


# Love

Love is a feeling of warmth inside,
Love is a gentle breeze,
Love is an emotion we cannot control,
Love is a part of my life.

Love is a feeling two people have,
Love is a warm, sunny day,
Love is an emotion we feel and we know,
Love is a part of my life.

**Leah Reid  (13)**
**Orangefield High School**

# Friends Poem

Friends are people
That love and care.
Friends are people
Who are always there.

If I ever need a friend
I could guarantee that
One would be there.

We could not live
Without our friends.
I want my friends
Till the every end.

**Claire Jackson  (14)**
**Orangefield High School**

# My Dog Jake

My dog is a loveable sort,
He's the mess in my room,
He puts the noise in noisy,
He's the sun for he always brightens up my day!
He's the smell from my socks,
He's like the fire on a winter's day.
He is as black as soot,
And he's the friend I will always have!

**Gemma Albert  (12)**
**Orangefield High School**

# My Family

My family is a happy family,
My dad is always glad.
My mum is always chewing gum,
My brothers are pests, but they are the best.

My family, my family, are all so different.
One has black hair, one has blonde,
One has a bad temper,
But I don't mind.
One is cheeky, not like me,
The only thing in common is our second name!

**Ryan McCormack  (14)**
**Orangefield High School**


# Seasons

Spring, it is so beautiful and all
The birds and flowers are wonderful.
Cold it is, but I won't fear,
Because summer will soon be near.
Let's go on holiday, get a good tan.
It's fading away and so is the sun,
Autumn is here, all the leaves are falling of the trees.
It's wet and cold again.
Winter is approaching very quickly,
It's snowing and Christmas will be here.
Winter is nearly over and it's all going to happen again.

**Nicola McNeill  (13)**
**Orangefield High School**

# My New Pet

I have a new cat, she is called Tigger.
She bounces and hops, runs and stalks,
She plays and sleeps.
She steals bacon from the grill
And chases Evil Eevee around the house.
She plays with fake mice
And any other moving things.
Tigger's her name and she is very cute.
She is very cuddly, but watch out,
She will eat your feet.

**David Ross  (14)**
**Orangefield High School**


# Jake

My dog Jake is as black as night,
Runs as fast as a crack of a whip.
He is sometimes as funny as a clown.
He sunbathes on sunny days and
Hides away on rainy days.
Sometimes he's in a good mood, or sometimes bad,
But I love him whatever mood he's in.
He's the sail on a boat, or an engine in a car,
But he's the best dog by far.

**Jonathan Albert  (12)**
**Orangefield High School**

# My Dog Rosie

My dog is called Rosie,
My sister calls her Rosie Posie.
I just have to laugh,
I laughed when the dog trailed her down the path.

My brother feeds the dog because I hate the smell,
I hate when her bells go jing-a-ling.

I love my dog Rosie, she is mostly mine,
I got her for my birthday when I was nine.
She is a Bichon Frise and I call her Fluffy Ball,
Because she is so fluffy and white and small.

**Leah Spiers  (11)**
**Orangefield High School**


# The Weather Poem

Weather, weather, make up your mind today.
Are you going to rain or shine?
I wonder what it will do today?
If you are sunny, I will be happy and cheerful.
If you are raining, I will be sad and grumpy.

So come on weather, get your act together,
Make it nice and sunny so that everyone is happy.
Weather, weather, make my day,
Make it sunny and warm today.

**Christopher Hutchinson  (13)**
**Orangefield High School**

# Birthday Thank Yous

Dear Auntie,
Oh what a nice toothbrush,
I've always wanted a blue one,
And fancy you thinking of toothpaste too,
How clever of you!

Dear Granny,
The dress is terrific, the Barbie-pink suits me to a tee,
And it matches the pink shoes
You bought me last year,
How thoughtful of you.

Dear Grandad,
Thanks for the tissues,
The dark green reminds me of you,
Now I can't wait for the flu.

Dear Dad,
What a wonderful present,
I can't say thank you enough.
You didn't have to choose,
I could have done that for you,
My own mobile!

**Janine Ingram   (13)**
**Parkhall College**

# My First Day

At first I was afraid of starting big school,
But by the end of the day, I thought it was quite cool.
Some of the teachers are really nice,
Others give you homework and treat you like mice.
PE is a blast, we have lots of fun,
But all we seem to do is run, run, run.
All the other subjects and classes are boring,
Because all we seem to do is writing and drawing.
I loved the start of the year,
At first I was afraid, but now I've lost my fear.

**Rachel Arthur   (12)**
**Parkhall College**

# My New Start

Summer holidays gone with a blast,
The day I've been waiting for is here at last.
Secondary school here I come,
Oh I do hope it's going to be fun.

Waiting for the bus, tummy full of nerves,
Up and down hills as well as round curves.
Tummy nerves going into a ball
When I finally see the sign for Parkhall.

The wheels on the bus get slower and slower,
Eventually it moves no more.
You can only hear the thump of my heart,
Because we're finally here at my new start.

**Donna Cooper  (13)**
**Parkhall College**


# My Dog Ben

My dog is Ben
Who enjoys chasing hens.
When not doing that,
He enjoys chasing cats.

And when not doing that,
He enjoys chasing taxmen.
Who would complain?

And when not doing that,
He chases the postman,
Who would complain?
The bills have been eaten,
Who would complain?

**Robert Graham  (12)**
**Parkhall College**

# My Mum

My mum brings me lots of joy.
She has a warming heart,
A glowing smile,
Which cheers me when I'm down.

My mum does many wonderful things,
She cares for me,
She loves me,
She's there for me.

My mum is many things,
She's my mum who cares for me,
She's my friend who's there for me,
She's beautiful.
So now I can safely say,
My mum is wonderful in every way.

**Angela Lynch (13)**
**Parkhall College**


# Dad

You are always there when I need you,
You are always there when I'm in trouble,
You are always there to provide for me,
You are always there to spoil me rotten,
You are always there to talk to,
You are always there to shout for me,
You are always there to feed me,
You are always there to school me,
You are always there to have fun with,
You are always there to take me places,
You are always there to say thank you to.

**Toni McCrubb (12)**
**Parkhall College**

# Dad, Where Are You?

I lie at night and think about you,
Walking about thinking it through.
Thinking to myself, *why?*
I realise how fly

I come to a halt
And think it is my fault
That my father is gone.
I need a magic wand.

I think back through the years,
There they come, all my tears.
I'm all alone, all alone on the streets,
Nothing to do but go to sleep.

All the memories floating around,
Places aren't as good as found.
Why can't he come back?
I see all his stuff packed.

Calling out to you,
Where are you?
Please, please, please,
Make this ease.

**Stacey McLaughlin  (13)**
**Parkhall College**

# The Lost Man

The man is lost,
He asks his way
From a woman passing,
Who can't delay.

Not quite sure
The route you should take,
Ask someone else,
For goodness sake.

The man is lost,
He asks his way
From a chap on the corner,
Who just bids him good day.

He wanders the streets,
Hour after hour,
Sweats in the sun
And gets soaked in the showers.
The poor old man.

**Jamie Steele (12)**
**Parkhall College**


# I Love Trains

I love trains,
Bump after bump,
I always jump,
Bouncing up and down
Like a clown.
The horn goes *toot*
It goes faster and faster,
You look out of the window
To see what you can see.
And when it stops,
Your ears go *pop*
And the wheels go *squeak*.
I love trains.

**Glenn Galloway (12)**
**Parkhall College**

# Shrek

Once upon a time,
In a wood dark and grim,
There was a monster named Shrek,
Who had a cheesy grin.

This monster was Scottish,
A friendly kind of bloke,
But the people didn't think so,
They wanted him choked.

There was a king who tried to kill
The monster by the name of Shrek.
Ooh, but then did he realise
He'd made a stupid mistake.

There you go, kids,
That's all from this fairy tale.
Wasn't that an interesting story
That has been told?

Especially by a twelve-year-old.

**Grant Simpson  (12)**
**Parkhall College**


# Castles

Yo, my name is Rick,
I build castles with brick.
First I build a wall,
About two metres tall,
Then I build a keep
On a hill that is steep.
In come the men
In rows of ten,
Well, they guarded it good,
And so they should.
It wall fall down one day,
Because I built it faulty anyway!

**Adam Coyle  (12)**
**Parkhall College**

## My Dog

My dog is called Spike,
Who always likes to bite,
And when we take him for a walk,
We always take him to the park.

Spike is so white,
He's always out of sight
And when he comes back,
We give him a snack.

When he is sad
He gets really mad
And makes a mess
While I'm getting dressed.

**Samantha Milligan  (12)**
**Parkhall College**


## The Match

As the teams wait in the tunnel,
Their nerves grow greater.
They listen to the crowd's roars
As they walk onto the field.
They stand in a line, sing and shake hands,
When the game starts, they're like rival gangs.

They kick the ball up the field from player to player,
The ball ends up in the net.
What? That's the whistle for half-time.

The players walk onto the pitch again for the second half,
Once again the ball is kicked from player to player.
It ends up in the net, twice again.
That's the whistle for full-time.
Some happy shouts erupt . . . but look at those sad faces.

**Simon Adams  (12)**
**Parkhall College**

# Goodbye

My mother is very sick,
I think she's going to die,
All I want to do is sit and cry.
I think she has cancer,
I am really very sad.
I want her to stay beside me
For all time.
I don't want her to die,
She's my mum.
She's my best, best friend.

Now she's gone,
I'm left all alone.
I'm very sad,
Will you be my new best friend?

**Roisin Higgins (11)**
**St Louise's College, Belfast**


# My Best Things

Sweets, crisps,
Animals too,
Teacher says they aren't good for you.
Ice cream and jelly,
I love things on the telly.
Holidays by the sea,
How better could it be?
Don't like school,
It's not cool,
Only in technology
When you get to use a tool.

**Ashling McCabe (11)**
**St Louise's College, Belfast**

# Hallowe'en

Hairy spiders creep about
You never know what might pop out.

Out in the dark where nobody goes,
There's a great big goblin picking his nose.

Witches on brooms, flying so high,
Watching their cats leap in the sky.

Down in the graveyard late at night,
Ghosts and skeletons give you a fright.

Down the street hear a creak,
It's the thumping of bodies dancing to a beat.

Dressed in Hallowe'en costumes, going trick or treat,
Holding Mummy's hand while walking down the street.

Pumpkin pie and candy apples, fireworks shooting in the sky,
It's nearly dawn, so it's time to say goodbye.

The skeletons, witches, goblins and children have all gone to sleep.
Shh, wait till next year to see where we creep!

**Kerriann Nesbitt (11)**
**St Louise's College, Belfast**

# The Stranger

The stranger wants to come and play,
But everybody ran away.

He wanders lonely about the streets,
No one to play with, nothing to eat.

He knocks on doors, he holds his side,
The folk inside just run and hide.

Now he knows he's far too old,
He's left alone, out in the cold.

**Orlaith Lynn (12)**
**St Louise's College, Belfast**

# What Is A Friend?

A friend is someone special,
Always there when you're in need.
They always will believe you,
And that is true indeed.

If you need some comfort,
Something you need to say,
A friend will always listen,
Even if she knows anyway.

If I am scared or worried
And need someone to pick me up,
She will always be there,
Even if there's nothing wrong.

My friend is so important,
I would never let her go.
She is someone special,
That I will always know.

**Anna Growcott (11)**
**St Louise's College, Belfast**


# My Best Things

Coke and sweets and honey,
And lots of money.
Rings and bracelets and my mobile too,
Saturday mornings are good for you!

I like the cold side of the pillow,
When I have a good dream,
After a bowl of ice cream.

I love Christmas, I love a dare,
And a trick, but I don't *care!*

**Roisin Campbell**
**St Louise's College, Belfast**

# My Best Things

Coke from the fridge, sausage rolls,
My breakfast in a big bowl.
My pillow on the other side,
Going down a big, big slide,
Strawberry trifle with cream and jelly,
Practically everything that goes in my belly.
Horror, horror and loads of pop,
Begin on that, I will never stop.
A paper ball I love to flick,
Mentioning of coleslaw makes me sick,
Waking up on Christmas morning,
I love the feeling of just yawning.
My brother falling down the stairs,
Going on a school trip in pairs,
On trampolines I love to skip it,
An unexpected £10 note,
Going for a trip on a boat.
The thought of a new bike,
Now that's the things I like.
Chicken crispy from McDonald's in town,
Or getting a pound,
Chips and chicken from Sunday dinner,
Celtic becoming the league winner.
The end of days, weeks and terms,
The habit of little worms,
Getting a Slush Puppy on a warm day,
Waiting for Friday to get my pay.

Now I could go on forever.

**Jennifer McConnell  (11)**
**St Louise's College, Belfast**

# What A Feeling!

One little girl left her country
And she is known to be friendly.
She keeps on talking,
But nobody is listening.

As time went by,
She became shy.
Friends seem so far,
Just like a cold war.

They eat bread,
She eats rice,
For a moment she thought,
It was not so nice.

Her skin is dim as the dawn,
While others are as bright as day.
Nothing she could do as she sat down
Thinking of it, all in dismay.

Then one day a little girl sat beside her.
As they were eating their hamburger,
They shared their food with fun and laughter
As they were talking about their actor.

The girl realised she was not alone,
She didn't notice she was jumping for home.
Saying goodbye to the lonely feeling,
Her heart seems filled with joy never-ending.

**Denilee Vianzon (11)**
**St Louise's College, Belfast**

# The Rainbow

I love the rainbow so, so much,
It's colourful and bright,
And when it rains I'm looking
For a rainbow to come in sight.

I love to see the rainbow,
'Cause the rain's gone away,
It now means it's that special time
To go out, run and play.

The colours of the rainbow
Make me think of memories.
Happy days, sad days
And days full of glee.

I hope to see you, rainbow,
I hope we meet again,
For me you're very special,
Just like a special friend.

**Paula Gillen  (11)**
**St Louise's College, Belfast**


# My Best Things

My best thing is clothes,
I like to buy loads.
My best thing is jewellery,
I like to wear it regularly.

Music is my favourite thing,
But it's only when I sing.
I like to go to my English class,
But it's usually a task.

**Lisa Cole  (12)**
**St Louise's College, Belfast**

# My Best Things

A rainbow showing love,
A white flying dove,
Nice warm gloves,
Clear white snow,
Watching my favourite show,
Listening to a CD,
Playing on my PC.
I like sweets,
Going to my uncle Pete's.
I hate jelly,
But I love watching telly.
I hate the colour red
And I hate getting up out of my bed.

**Caitriona McKenna  (12)**
St Louise's College, Belfast


# Will You Still Be There?

If I get scared and lonely
Will you be there to hold my hand?

If I am getting bullied and am afraid to say,
Will you be there to hold my hand?

And when the skies are grey
And the sun can't break free,
Will you still be there to hold my hand?

And if I get dumped and I cry,
Please, please, say you'll be there to hold my hand.

**Dearbhla Cunningham  (11)**
St Louise's College, Belfast

# An Old Woman

At the back of the bookies' the old woman lingers,
Her eyes are saddened by abuse,
Smiling timidly, her mouth stretches from ear to ear.

The woman struggles to rise, she cries,
She sways her head aimlessly.
The print on her jacket fades.

She fidgets with her zip.
Her black slippers are torn,
Her toes are peeping through the holes.
She scratches her pimpled head.

She raises her hand to her chin,
She slants her head,
'What will become of me?' she sobs.

**Megan Doyle  (11)**
**St Louise's College, Belfast**


# My Pet

My pet is called Rocky.
He is tall, dark and brown,
He's got big, floppy ears that all droop down.

He runs round the garden like a great racing horse,
If he barks too much, he gets quite hoarse.

His paws are so big like a big, giant bear,
But I don't care, 'cause he's my great grizzly bear.

**Selene Ward  (11)**
**St Louise's College, Belfast**

# Hallowe'en Is Here!

H allowe'en is here
A nd the witches are out tonight.
L ittle children rapping doors and saying, 'Trick or treat?'
L anterns hanging from door to door,
O h! Look at the moon shining bright.
W ill I ever see another scary night?
E vil screams and cackles are coming,
E veryone hide and don't walk alone.
N ight is going and everything is fading,
    I hope this night won't ever come.

**Kerryann Auld (11)**
**St Louise's College, Belfast**


# Dogs

I love dogs so very much,
They're so cute and cuddly,
I think they're quite lush.

Their eyes are beautiful,
Their ears are wonderful,
There are big ones, small ones,
Skinny ones and tall ones.

I love boxers, huskies and
Cute puppy-dogs,
I hate when they do their mysterious logs!

**Aoife Nolan (11)**
**St Louise's College, Belfast**

# I Hate

I hate having the flu,
Walking by seeing dogs' poo.
People killing, people dying,
Children falling, babies crying.

Rangers winning the Scottish cup,
People screaming, 'Ha, ha, bad luck.'
Having homework piled to the top,
Walking to class, being told to stop.

Tests on subjects I don't like,
My tyres going flat on my new bike,
Being told to be quiet by my big brother,
Who's nothing like my kind, loving mother.

I hope you liked my poem on this I hate,
Remember to do your homework
And don't go to bed too late.

**Lorrin Edgar  (11)**
**St Louise's College, Belfast**